Peer-to-Peer Culture

What It Takes for Small Businesses To Grow Up

Mark Budzinski

ISBN: 9798664236729

© 2020 by Mark Budzinski

Edition 1.0

Peer-to-Peer Culture™ is a trademark of Mark Budzinski. All other trademarks are property of their respective owners.

All rights reserved. This work may not be translated or copied in whole or in part without the written permission of the publisher, except for brief excerpts in connection with reviews or scholarly analysis. Use in connection with any form of information storage and retrieval, electronic adaptation, computer software, or by similar or dissimilar methodology now known or hereafter developed is forbidden.

To My Love

Table of Contents

PREFACE	III
GROWING UP IS HARD	1
CULTURE IN THEORY	15
CULTURE IN PRACTICE	33
THE 5 ATTRIBUTES OF PEER-TO-PEER CULTURE	51
Trust	53
Team Orientation	73
Empathy	87
Honesty	105
Dynamic Action	121
STRUCTURING THE PEER-TO-PEER ORGANIZATION	139
MANAGING THE PEER-TO-PEER ORGANIZATION	155
HIRING AND ASSIMILATION	169
EXTENDING PEER-TO-PEER TO CUSTOMERS	183
EPILOGUE	197

Table of Figures

Figure 1: Startup Culture Is Organic	3
Figure 2: Growing Up Is Hard	6
Figure 3: Where Values and Behavior Meet	11
Figure 4: What We Say Is Not What We Do	20
Figure 5: Propaganda Versus Reality	25
Figure 6: Roles and People	27
Figure 7: Transparent Agreement	36
Figure 8: Peer-to-Peer Culture	38
Figure 9: Peer-to-Peer Accountability	44
Figure 10: The Dilemma of Trust	62
Figure 11: How to Install Trust	66
Figure 12: The Circle of Trust	68
Figure 13: Blame and Action	74
Figure 14: The Elusive Scoreboard	80
Figure 15: Peer-to-Peer Scoreboard	83
Figure 16: How to Install Teamwork	85
Figure 17: Carl Rogers' Approach	91
Figure 18: Alternatives in Negotiation	93
Figure 19: Micro-Agreements	100
Figure 20: How to Install Empathy	102
Figure 21: Model Penal Code	112
Figure 22: Honesty Is Not Ruthless	113
Figure 23: A Stale Sandwich	115
Figure 24: Peer-to-Peer Honesty	116
Figure 25: Maslow's Hierarchy	125
Figure 26: TRACOM® SOCIAL STYLE Model™	132
Figure 27: Direct Communication	134
Figure 28: Cross-Functional Initiatives	144
Figure 29: Common Pay Plan	148
Figure 30: Peer-to-Peer Pay Plan	151
Figure 31: Common Corporate Policy	157
Figure 32: Managing Employee Performance	162
Figure 33: Peer-to-Peer Hiring Matrix	171

Figure 34: Assimilation 179
Figure 35: Realpolitik Comparison 185
Figure 36: Wilsonian Comparison 189
Figure 37: Evolution of Customer Behavior 191

Preface

What do you believe about business, and why do you believe it? These are intriguing questions. If you are prepared to reflect honestly, then you are well-placed to read on.

Leading a company through the transition from $5 million to $50 million USD in annual revenue is a trying undertaking. I know because I engaged in the challenge. As a CEO, I led a firm with revenues toward the bottom of that range to something closer to the top in a few years. The investors were able to exit in a lucrative fashion, opening up a chance for a fresh set of owners to initiate their journey.

Successful as it was, the path to prosperity was anything but prescribed, planned, or well-conceived. For a good while, chaos reigned. In fact, before being elevated to CEO, I was a willing participant in this company, helping to perpetuate the chaos in a variety of roles. Working for the founders, I assembled a small team to grow the business in the United States, while a colleague got the first set of customers off the ground in Europe. When the colleague departed, and I added the European business to my plate.

It was day-to-day, hand-to-hand combat to pursue prospective customers, engage in successful sales campaigns, close business, and service the customer after the sale. We all did whatever we had to do, day or night, weekday, or weekend, to make it happen. Something must have worked because the business grew at a nice, steady clip. We attracted new institutional investors, the founders resigned from their operational roles, and I embraced the opportunity to lead the company outright as chief executive officer. My objective would be to grow the company to the next mid-level size, as measured by revenue, sustained profitability, and operational footprint, so that investors could exit successfully.

Upon my assignment as a new CEO, and as the journey commenced, the cues for what exactly I should do to enrich our chances for a favorable outcome were plentiful. In fact, they were probably too plentiful.

On the one hand, the company was well-entrenched in a kindred spirit and a way of operating effective since the startup days. We had good products and hundreds of happy customers. Many of the original staff, along with their ad hoc processes, were in place and thriving. Their contributions were invaluable.

On the other hand, we faced a whole slew of operational challenges. As nimble as we were to satisfy any given customer, clinging to whatever informal process was required, we had inadequate ability to read market signals more broadly, comprehend competitive forces, and act decisively. The product sold to our first customers during the company's outset was still an important part of the portfolio but was showing signs of aging. Should we continue to invest in its evolution, or replace it with newer products?

On top of it all, the institutional investors insisted that the company had to mature with respect to policy, governance, and formal organizational structure that larger firms maintain. They led talk of exit strategies and revenue multiples. Their mandate was to grow up as a company as much as grow our top line.

It was not long before I realized that I was caught in a tug-of-war. The board of directors was pulling one way, the staff was tugging the other. Clearly, I was the rope.

To continue to operate as we were doing offered little hope for accelerated growth. The business was chugging along fine, but I could not, in its current form, forecast increases in revenue to meet more aggressive expectations. Yet, to be seduced by investor-led advice, formulas, and opinions did not appeal to me, either. They meant well, certainly, but were not in touch with the subtleties and nuances of the business. To install their wishes verbatim would have been risky at best, perhaps disastrous.

I decided to engage a set of colleagues who would help me. It would be a small set, only five or six. And the choice was not a decision to be made lightly. It was a bet, really. Who I selected to join me in the endeavor would form the foundation of everything we would do. I had to get it right. I settled on one basic criterion: trust.

It was a trust in demonstrated aptitude, certainly. Those selected maintained general skills such as problem-solving and people management, as well as functional competence at a high level. But it was more a trust in character. This group would be asked to sign up for the challenge with the same unwavering degree of commitment as I had. Traits of initiative and perseverance were paramount. But it was the commitment to clear communication, which I held most dear, that would underpin our trust. No posturing. No BS. I craved people with whom I could be direct and honest, without reservation, and who would behave the same way with me.

Within the framework of direct and open communication, I gave my trust explicitly and proactively to the group I selected. And I asked for theirs in return. It was an unequivocal agreement, stated right out loud.

Essentially, we defined a company culture. We called it peer-to-peer, the subject under the hot lights in this book. We were to treat each other as peers, as equals, with an emphasis on authenticity. We would bring our "real selves" to the office, rejecting any temptation to mask personal agendas, fears, or desires. We would talk about it all, transparently, as a routine part of our professional conduct.

And when it came to our customers, we would strive to behave the same way. We would be honest and straightforward in our approach to acquiring customers from the first encounter, through to the sale, and thereafter in our ongoing relationship. We would emphasize the notion of teamwork in setting and achieving goals. Truly "in it together," we decided to win as a team and lose as a team, always.

The results we savored from the installed peer-to-peer culture were extraordinary. Revenue and profitability goals were smashed. Employee morale was through the roof. Customer satisfaction and trust in their vendor were unprecedented. Did our approach to corporate culture and our downstream systems and policy fully explain our success? Unlikely. Luck always plays a part. But any leader worth their salt will confess that putting a group in the best possible position to be lucky is crucial. Make your own luck, as the saying goes. The result, as my three-year tenure concluded, was a successful exit for shareholders.

Although the key ideas explored in this book come largely from my time spent operating a company offering products and services in the business-to-business paradigm, the concepts put forth apply to business-to-consumer firms as well.

My points might clash with much of what you think about corporate culture. Indeed, if I am successful in my intent, managers operating companies in all genres and industries will be provoked and challenged.

If you are an executive, or senior manager in a growing, emerging organization, I am addressing my remarks to you. But in truth, this book is for all people who care about business and want to immerse themselves for a couple of hours in a thoughtful exercise to consider how the dynamics of human experience intersect with the abstract idea we call "a company."

I acknowledge and appreciate the many who helped me throughout my journey. Thanks to Stacey, Garrett, Savannah, Anna, Joe, Neil, Chris, Doug, Tantrum, Armon, Jason, Raphael, Tom Byrd PB, and Trainer John. To my No. 1 fan, my mom, and all the family on both sides of the aisle who have been superb throughout this process.

A special thanks to Marc, Anna, and Kathy for the great editing, and to David for the cover. Thanks to Michael and

Wayne for the opportunity and your trust. To John, for encouraging me to put my big-boy pants on.

But mostly, it was the devoted team I worked with over the last several years who inspired me, shaped my thinking, and rewarded me with such pleasure. What a joy it was to work with Kiwis, Brits, Singaporeans, Nederlanders, les Belges, Deutschen, Punekars, and, last but not least, Americans.

To all of you, I will always be grateful.

Mark Budzinski

July 2020

Growing Up Is Hard

Ask any founder of a company how they feel about what they have accomplished, and it's likely you'll hear a tone of satisfaction. From the seed of an idea, entrepreneurs can germinate a beautiful plant with flowering revenue supported by living, breathing organisms in the form of customers, staff, and partners.

It is a profound statement in support of the theories, professed all those years ago by Adam Smith, that people are able to create wealth from seemingly nothing.

But founders will also tell you that emotional stress and monumental intellectual challenges are omnipresent along the way. They must maintain steadfast belief and persevere through adversity. No one would classify the affair as easy, regardless of how marvelous the business idea appears at the outset.

Without any reservations, I admire and respect those who have done it. If you are one of them, congratulations. You are among a very small and revered group.

Success requires founders and their newly hired staff to behave with urgency, trust, and transparency. There is not much time for musing, much less wasted energy.

But as the company grows, coping mechanisms invariably emerge, leading to habits — good and bad — that quickly embed themselves as methods and processes. For example, how are decisions made? Does the founder behave autocratically, delegate, or collaborate and debate before reaching an outcome? How are prospective customers identified and pursued? When a product fails or a service goes awry, what remedies are prescribed? All of these questions, and more like them, must be confronted and resolved in short order or the startup stalls — or, in the worst case, ceases to exist. However informal or ad hoc they might be, the habits become ingrained.

Furthermore, while the managers focus on operational execution in pursuit of legitimacy, growth, and sustainability, a set of cultural elements materialize. They always do. Employees and customers will observe these elements in the form of management behavior and the perceived values that attach themselves.

Is teamwork exalted, for example, or does the firm motivate and reward individual contributions? Or, consider when things go wrong and a customer escalates an issue related to their dissatisfaction. Do blame and scapegoating tendencies emerge, or does the organization stay focused on seeking remedies and solutions without concern for retribution against those accountable for the problem?

Founders of a startup may be very explicit about the key components they wish to embrace in their corporate culture. Plaques in the lobby, websites, and press releases may include specific language describing the desired state of being. Posters may list "Our top 5 values," for example. But usually, it's all just a distraction.

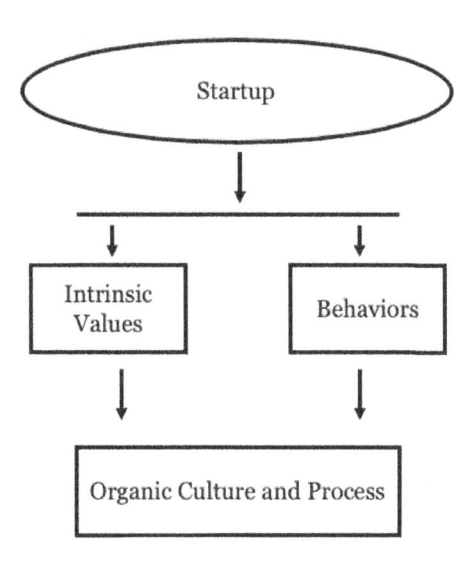

```
        ┌─────────┐
        │ Startup │
        └────┬────┘
             ↓
   ┌─────────┴─────────┐
   ↓                   ↓
┌─────────┐       ┌──────────┐
│Intrinsic│       │Behaviors │
│ Values  │       │          │
└────┬────┘       └────┬─────┘
     ↓                 ↓
   ┌─────────────────────┐
   │Organic Culture and Process│
   └─────────────────────┘
```

Figure 1: Startup Culture Is Organic

The evolution of corporate culture for the startup is more surreptitious, as the demands of the business can force the collective organization into a set of de facto, unconscious behavioral patterns. Leaders maintain intrinsic values, often unstated, that motivate their behavior. New employees observe then emulate the behavior. And before long, these behaviors often persist to frame a company culture.

It works much the same way with customers. Consider how a customer experiences their interaction with a new vendor throughout the purchasing life cycle. As a customer makes first contact, they engage in an educational process and entertain potential scenarios in which purchase of the product or service may be deemed worthy. Perhaps some level of due diligence is completed to validate legitimacy and address lingering perceptions of risk. Once the purchasing decision is made, the customer's focus moves swiftly to ensure satisfaction in installation, implementation, and integration of the product or service.

From the vendor's point of view, a startup will often introduce a small group of employees, perhaps even just one person, to engage in all of these steps of the customer journey, from pre- to post-sale. The level of care on display is extraordinarily high, as everyone involved realizes what is at stake. And the cultural attributes of the organization, exposed through this process, are often close to, if not entirely identical, to the values held by the founders themselves.

If the founders are honest and straight shooters, then the customer will experience their new vendor as candid and forthright. If the founders are cautious, and careful to manage assumptions and assurances in advance, customers will likely perceive the experience as equally measured and enjoy a positive outcome consistent with their conservative and well-understood expectations.

It is all very tidy. In the early days of the business, the culture of the firm is largely a natural extension of the founders' perspectives and values. The culture becomes observable then, in the form of their behavior. The initial set of managers and employees join the firm, watch the way founders behave, and follow suit. This core group directly introduces the cultural attributes of the firms they create, knowingly or not.

But once a startup finds initial success, a whole new set of challenges materialize. Founders need more staff, and more staff demands more managers. Process begets more process, and complexity mounts. Before long, the once presumed ability of the founding team to control matters becomes extremely difficult. In fact, never mind control. It becomes difficult to even retain awareness of all of the day-to-day issues, as new staff are hired and manage their tasks on a more specialized basis. Success and growth are fantastic. But the chaos? Yikes.

It is at this precise stage that a stubborn question finds life and requires a timely response: What do we do now?

This Is Going to Be Hard

The alluring journey is fraught with danger. A substantial number of firms that attempt the undertaking simply do not make it to the other side. Consider the facts: In the United States (as of March 2020) the number of businesses with annual sales greater than $500,000 USD but under $10 million was approximately 1.8 million[1].

Yet the count for businesses with at least $10 million but smaller than $100 million was roughly 189,000. In other words, for every firm with greater than $10 million in annual sales, there were about 10 who had achieved revenues greater than $500,000.

If we take this data at face value and extrapolate over time, we might infer that the probability of successfully growing

---

[1] https://www.naics.com/business-lists/counts-by-company-size/ March 2020 data

beyond $10 million is a modest 10%. And that does not even count the 13 million businesses under $500,000 in annual revenue. If that group is considered in the calculus, the probability of growing to $10 million drops to a scary low: slightly above 1%.

Of course, we can't get too carried away when making precise predictions about the future. But the data presented certainly offer a clue. Each stage of success presents challenges such that the probability of failure increases by an order of magnitude. Indeed, it is genuinely difficult to grow a business beyond the startup years. There is no doubt about it.

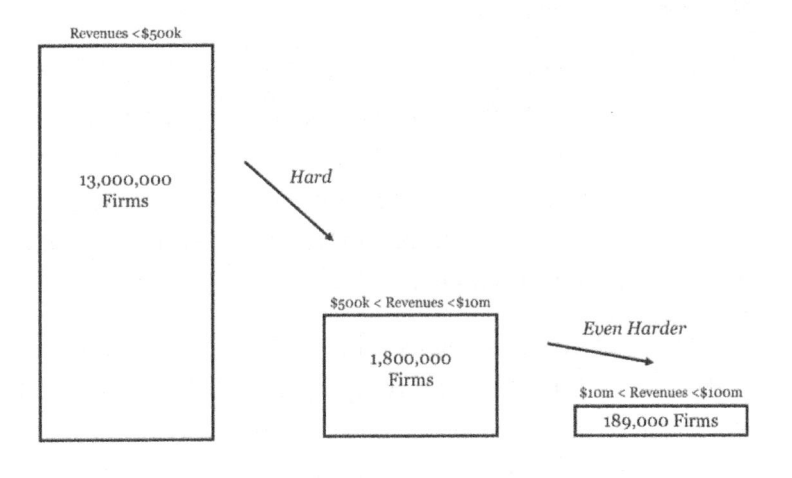

```
Revenues <$500k

┌─────────────┐
│             │
│             │
│ 13,000,000  │    Hard
│   Firms     │ ╲
│             │  ╲
│             │   ╲   $500k < Revenues <$10m
│             │    ╲ ┌──────────────┐
│             │      │              │       Even Harder
│             │      │  1,800,000   │ ──────────────►
│             │      │    Firms     │   $10m < Revenues <$100m
│             │      │              │   ┌──────────────┐
│             │      │              │   │ 189,000 Firms│
└─────────────┘      └──────────────┘   └──────────────┘
```

Figure 2: Growing Up Is Hard

Managers and employees of some firms are content to remain small indefinitely, throwing off cash to their principals in the fashion of the classic "lifestyle" company. Others are anxious to sell out, liquidate the firm's value, and leave it to others to figure out the best way forward.

Many, though, desire to continue the expedition and grow the firm they started through the next, potentially very lucrative intermediate stage. They want to leave the startup days behind and grow the company in sustainable, material terms. What was a few million dollars of annual revenue is now targeted for something substantially higher, perhaps $40 million, $50 million or more. And, if institutional investors are present in the undertaking, then surely such expectations persist with clarity and passion. Ambition is the watchword.

As a company's leaders answer the question, "What do we do now?" with conviction and express their ambition to grow the firm to midlevel success, the question now turns to, "How?" How, exactly, should they proceed?

It is tempting for executives and managers, wanting to grow to an intermediate stage, to rush to imitate the methods and processes on display in larger, more mature firms. It seems like the right thing to do. It's a seductive idea to look like them and behave like them in an effort to grow to be like them.

Big firms are not all the same, of course. But they often exhibit many of the same attributes. Most practice rigor and discipline in their approach to business processes. Information systems are installed, facilitating the execution of everything from customer relationship management to accounting. Organizational charts define the roles for employees, while managers serve to hold the staff accountable for a job well done.

Mainstream management doctrine such as key performance indicators (KPIs) are used to link individual performance to the group, and the group to corporate goals. And it is not uncommon to find schemes such as objectives and key results (OKRs) installed to call out goals and the corresponding criteria for achievement in the context of departmental and companywide objectives. When I joined Intel in 1983 as a new college grad, Andy Grove, the company's co-founder and a true Renaissance man, had installed just such a system, long before the current hype found on management consultant websites.

These big company practices are something to admire and apply. Management discipline is a good thing, generally speaking.

But before running to implement the big company manual verbatim, let's pause. Many of the formal elements of process and policy as espoused by successful managers of larger firms are inconsistent with the way most startups have achieved success to date. In fact, in many cases it is because the startup behaves with such informal process that the firm enjoys a nimble, responsive, competitive advantage. Now that they want to scale, the world is telling them to formalize.

I agree. But it's *what* you formalize that matters. Don't stress about formalizing process. Don't become obsessive about formalizing roles and drawing org charts. And certainly, don't get hyper-focused on KPIs, OKRs, and all the other chatter promoted by consultants. Formalize behavior. The necessary formalization of processes and roles will materialize *out* of formalized behavior. People will define the processes that need defining in a natural rhythm.

Setting the Course for Behavior

The question that I ponder isn't so much about how to implement new, documented, more rigorous processes to scale a company. The better question is how, exactly, to preserve the best elements of what got the company this far, while setting the organization up for success as growth takes hold. In other words, how does the small company with an appetite for bigger success evolve without breaking something in a way that proves fatal?

As I began my personal journey as CEO, we confronted many of the challenges seen by other firms embarking on the same voyage. There was nothing terribly unique about our situation. We lacked sophistication as an organization. Business processes were undocumented or nonexistent. New-hire assimilation was inconsistent up and down the org chart. And, with new institutional investors at the table, we had to develop a new taste for corporate policy and governance.

The young company that I was given the opportunity to lead was also undoubtedly like other small firms in the way tenured staff viewed change. The "old-timers," in our case, held a variety of positions ranging from individual contributor to senior manager. And collectively, they had convinced themselves that the way they operated was, though informal, very effective. Much of the day-to-day execution was done on a first-name basis.

If a customer, for example, encountered an obstacle to their satisfaction with our product, they would call whoever they knew in the organization to escalate the problem. Sometimes this was Bob, the salesperson. Or it could be Bill, the technical field resource that the customer got to know during the sales process. Or it might be Jane at the support desk. Whoever got the call made the real-time, basic decision of what to do with the customer's issue. Bob might ring Bill in an attempt to get somebody with technical skills on the case. Or Jane might email Mary Lou in the product development team and ask questions about any number of details. Everyone behaved, as they saw it, in the best interest of the customer. And as it turns out, customer issues *were* usually resolved. But the time wasted in the thrashing was obviously undesirable and undeniably unsustainable if we were to prosper.

When I confronted the staff, they readily admitted that spontaneous implementation of ad hoc, organically defined process was not ideal. And they understood that to grow the company, we needed to behave with more discipline.

But when it came down to it, the prospect of doing things differently scared everyone. Memories from time with previous employers over the course of people's careers sprang forth, holding traffic signs that said, "Caution," "Stop," "Proceed at your own risk."

Change, in other words, suited everyone in the abstract. But implementation was another matter. It was tempting to view the problems as tactical and go at them one by one: How do we improve this or that? The problem set was overwhelming.

I came to realize that operational change, however logical, was laden with risk. I had to find some form of bedrock that would serve as an unmovable, reliable foundation upon which the staff could rely. Operational change could only be built on such a foundation. We would come to call this foundation "culture."

I surrounded myself with a small group of competent co-pilots who shared my enthusiasm for culture. We gave the subject a disproportionately large amount of our collective bandwidth, focus, and intellect from the very outset when we took control of the company.

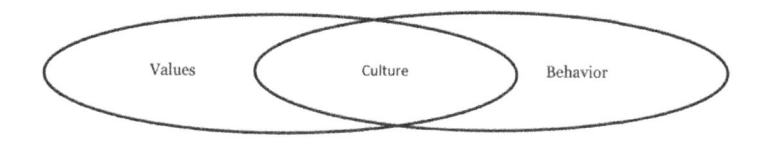

Figure 3: Where Values and Behavior Meet

Our culture had to be defined by behavior, underpinned by values. To simply assert a set of desired values, without defining corresponding behavioral expectations, would merely be a feel-good rhetorical exercise. The last thing we wanted was a useless plaque on the wall with a bunch of righteous descriptors of morality. But, to bark out a set of desired behaviors, without a direct connection to value-based principles, would be equally obtuse. The two were intertwined. Values underpin behavior, while tangible acts of behavior must exhibit desired values. Together, they define culture.

I find this notion powerful. Culture — the foundation of an enterprise — should not be difficult to install, administer, or regulate. When a culture is defined as the intersection of values and behavior, people either behave correctly or they don't. And when they don't, we can fix it. Ill-intended people can be removed, while simple misunderstandings can lead to rehabilitation and a renewed commitment to the correct, desired behavior.

The stakes we faced in our company were high. Culture, in the end, was going to be the key to success.

In Sum

- Successful new companies, more often than not, require founders and their immediate set of newly hired staff to behave with urgency, trust, and transparency.

- Leaders of early-stage companies maintain intrinsic values, often unstated, that motivate their behavior. Employees observe then emulate the behavior. Before long, these behaviors persist to frame a company culture.

- History suggests that it is genuinely difficult to grow a business beyond the startup years. Most organizations that have tried have failed.

- It is tempting for executives and managers who desire to grow to an intermediate stage to rush to adopt methods and processes on display in larger, more mature firms.

- Many of the formal elements of process and policy as espoused by successful managers of larger firms are inconsistent with the way most startups have achieved their initial success.

- To scale a business, it is what you formalize that matters. Formalize behavior.

- When a culture is defined as the intersection of values and behavior, people either behave correctly or they don't. And when they don't, we can fix it.

Culture in Theory

We are, of course, familiar with the term "culture" from sociology and our observations of everyday life. I particularly like the way Yuval Noah Harari talks about culture in his book *Sapiens: A Brief History of Humankind*[2]. Harari describes how groups of people who are destined to cooperate invent "imagined realities," which, tethered to the resulting behavior patterns, form the basic components of culture.

Cultures have changed and developed for groups of people throughout human history, whether they be communities, religious groups, or nations. A company that engages employees, partners, and customers is like any other group. It maintains a set of imagined realities, and the people involved all exhibit associated behavioral patterns.

Perhaps unsurprisingly, statements to describe culture are often conflated with a declared set of values. Certainly, nations such as the United States profess essential values such as "freedom" and "rights" that are familiar to the inhabitants. Religious groups may declare, "Do unto others as you would like others to do unto you," while secular groups may promote kindness and philanthropy.

A firm in business to make a profit is no different. A statement, or more likely a network of statements, is offered to define the

---

[2] Yuval N. Harari, *Sapiens: A Brief History of Humankind* (U.S. edition, HarperCollins, 2015). https://www.ynharari.com/book/sapiens/

value system of the enterprise to all audiences related to the firm's interests. Recall your own indoctrination into your employers over the course of your career. Perhaps the idea of corporate culture was delivered as oral testimony by someone in the human resources department or by your manager. You may have even received a manual. Did a poster greet you in the lobby on your first day in the office?

As one would imagine, it is in the best interest of the establishment to put forth proclamations that are viewed favorably by all audiences. Noble ideas of integrity and honesty often emerge. Senior management express ideas such as "doing the right thing" and "open door policy" as indicators of expectations for employees. Customers hear how their vendor strives to "delight" and "listen to" them. Not uncommonly, and with great fanfare, companies publish representations of their culture and the associated value system for public consumption.

Navigating the website of a typical firm today yields published pages such as Tableau's "Our Core Cultural Values: Who we are is as important as what we do."[3] The firm goes on to list the values as follows:

1. *We are on a mission.*
2. *We build great products.*
3. *We use our products.*
4. *We work as a team.*

---

[3] https://www.tableau.com/about/values

5. *We respect each other.*
6. *We are honest.*
7. *We keep it simple.*
8. *We delight our customers.*

Surely, this enumeration of feel-good statements is hard to argue with. If you are a customer, check the box. They will delight you. Are you an employee? Don't fret. Honesty and team orientation rule the day. Are you an investor? You will undoubtedly be fond of great products and a commitment to a clear mission.

Managers at IBM, a larger and more mature company, appear to have invested considerable thought in the way they articulate their values in more verbose terms on their website[4]:

At IBM, values mean more than ethics, compliance, or even a code of conduct.

Values express:

- *What differentiates IBM with clients, investors, employees, communities.*
- *Our mission, our aspirations.*
- *How we make decisions at our company.*
- *How we behave and act, collectively and individually.*

---

[4] https://www.ibm.com/ibm/values/us/

Our shared values in action:

1. *Dedication to every client's success.*

   IBMers...

   - *are passionate about building strong, long-lasting client relationships. This dedication spurs us to go "above and beyond" on our clients' behalf.*

   - *are focused on outcomes. We sell products, services, and solutions to help our clients succeed, however they measure success.*

   - *demonstrate this personal dedication to every client, from the largest corporation and government agency to the smallest organization.*

   - *no matter where they work, have a role in client success. It requires the full spectrum of IBM expertise.*

2. *Innovation that matters — for our company and for the world.*

   IBMers...

   - *are forward thinkers. We believe that the application of intelligence, reason and science can improve business, society, and the human condition.*

   - *love grand challenges, as well as everyday improvements. Whatever the problem or the context, every IBMer seeks ways to tackle it creatively — to be an innovator.*

- *strive to be first — in technology, in business, in responsible policy.*
- *take informed risks and champion new (sometimes unpopular) ideas.*

3. *Trust and personal responsibility in all relationships.*

   IBMers...

   - *actively build relationships with all the constituencies of our business — including clients, partners, communities, investors and fellow IBMers.*
   - *build trust by listening, following through, and keeping their word.*
   - *rely on our colleagues to do the right thing.*
   - *preserve trust even when formal relationships end.*

One reads this account and is left to consider, "Why wouldn't you want to buy from these guys?" The value system as documented approaches virtuousness, perhaps even righteousness. Trust and honesty, going above and beyond, and dedication are excellent descriptors of an ideal way of life by any moral standard.

But are statements of corporate culture consistent with actual experience in most companies?

Theory in Practice

In their insightful book *Theory in Practice,* Chris Argyris and Donald Schon articulate the distinction between espoused theory and theory in practice.[5] Simply stated, what people say they believe about themselves, and, by extension, what they want others to believe about them, is different, and often in conflict, with how they behave. Who they want you to think they are is often different from who they really are.

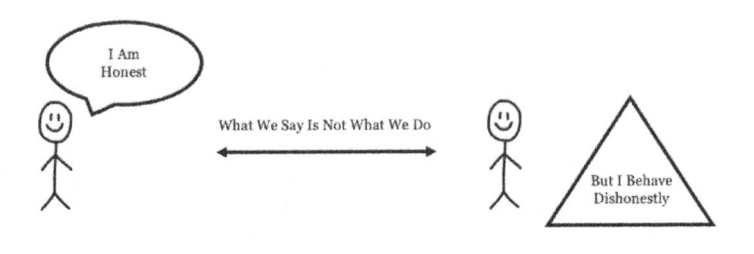

Figure 4: What We Say Is Not What We Do

This is crucially important. What we *say* — those lists of values that explain the culture in theory – is often not what we *do* — the culture in practice. In fact, what we say is often opposed to what we do, or, at best, is designed to provide air cover for what we do. We should stop shouting about who we are (e.g., the case with IBM) and start talking more about how we should be behaving with our fellow employees, customers, and suppliers. Internal behavior, practiced and observed

---

[5] Chris Argyris, Donald Schon, *Theory in Practice: Increasing Professional Effectiveness* (Jossey-Bass Publishers, 1974).

within the walls of the firm, forms the basis for external behavior practiced and observed with customers, partners, and others outside the firm.

I believe many corporate cultures offer a vivid example of the dissonance highlighted in Argyris and Schon's work. All too often, the poster doesn't match the prevailing behavior. The firm says it cherishes customers, but does it? The HR manual screams that employees are appreciated, and, by extension, their families are as well. But are they? What do we know about corporate culture from our own experiences as customers and employees?

Consider the way most customers engage with their vendors. Usually, three communication channels provide the platform: live interaction with the sales professional, email with the accounting office, and telephone calls with the support desk. In other words, customers deal with salespeople (and their supporting cast) to buy, are invoiced by accounting, and reach out to the support desk when something goes awry. The lucky customers (or those big enough to throw their weight around) also gain access to senior management for escalation and off-the-record dialogue.

If the culture in theory says, "Cherish the customer," how then do the people in the roles likely to interact with the customer behave as a cohesive unit to realize this objective? You can find examples galore in your own experience where breakdowns occur routinely. Customers buy with a set of expectations. If expectations aren't met, for whatever reason, salespeople and support teams must come together to resolve the issues and satisfy the customer. Does the support desk know what expectation was set by the salesperson during the buying cycle? Usually, they have no idea. And if issues remain unresolved for several weeks, how does the customer respond when hounded by the accounting office about late payment? We have a complete breakdown in our "cherish the customer" corporate value, yet it happens again and again. The poster in the lobby is rendered irrelevant. The customer experiences something far afield from being cherished.

How they buy, how they pay, and how they get help use three completely different communication channels, appearing to be from different companies. It is all innocent enough, but the consequences can be catastrophic. Clearly, a level of consistency in the way a customer is treated should qualify as a minimum standard for "cherishing the customer." Yet, by forcing the customer to interact with the firm through disparate channels, consistency goes awry and the culture in theory goes out the window.

Again, let's reflect on the early days of a firm's existence. In the startup phase, the face of the company as experienced by customers is singular. What gets sold and what gets delivered are tightly connected. But more importantly, *how* the customer interacts with the vendor pre-sale to post-sale is seamless, without handoff or abrupt interruption. In truth, this is a form of intimacy, as startups breed deep customer relationships.

Feeling the Impact of the Gap

Imagine how a customer feels when the vendor, while growing the enterprise, introduces new actors, new processes, and new human error to the relationship.

In essence, the vendor fragments and distributes the customer relationship. In fact, the vendor may be so preoccupied with its own efforts that it may not even recognize the problems it introduced. But the customer sees them, you can bet. And criticisms of, "Well, I guess the vendor is turning out to be just like all the rest of them" follow. For customers, it feels like a loss. They *want* intimacy in the relationship. When they stop getting it, it feels like heartbreak.

Espousing a corporate cultural value of "cherish the customer" in this scenario becomes indefensible, and potentially preposterous from the customer's perspective. The vendor's website declarations are reduced to rhetorical devices.

It becomes a blindness, in which the company cannot see its failures as distinct from espoused values. For example, a company's staff might over-position their remarks or even lie to customers in the name of intimacy. I have observed, earlier in my career, employees communicate to customers that *they*, and their department, have a unique positive regard for the customer. It must be *them*, the other department, that has screwed up the customer's shipment. In truth, these employees are practicing indifference rather than intimacy.

Employee experiences with each other are also often very different from those expected from championed values documented in the company manual. Management says they desire a state wherein the staff respect each other and work as a team.

Yet, when staff attend internal meetings, they find posturing (inflated self-promotion), defensive routines (cover your ass), and blaming others (throwing fellow employees under the bus) as dominating elements. Teamwork, though espoused as a component of corporate culture, gives way to a behavior in practice that is more adversarial. Again, I have seen it firsthand in my days in larger firms. When a key milestone is missed on a project schedule, for example, employees will make an excuse and pass blame, saying they didn't get what they needed, in time, from a colleague: "Wasn't my fault." The agendas of self-interest come at the expense of others.

So, which is it? Intimacy or indifference? Teamwork or adversarial behavior laced with self-interest?

In these scenarios, the espoused culture simply does not match the culture in practice and the actual behavior experienced by staff and customers. A firm will say it cherishes customers but behave with indifference and inconsistency. Managers say they value teamwork but set up an environment that encourages adversarial relationships and rewards individual achievement.

Given the gap between rhetoric and practice, I am left to believe that management teams at larger firms resist, fail to recognize, or perhaps entirely ignore the opportunity for resolving the dissonance. Furthermore, I wonder if we don't expect, and to some extent celebrate, a capacity in our senior leaders to press on even when they are keenly aware of *big* gaps between "what we say" and reality. It's a skill in tolerating cognitive dissonance that professional investors may even covet in their leaders. Regardless, I don't think our employees have that capacity. And neither do our customers.

As a standard matter of course, senior management dismissively assigns the duty of creating and sustaining corporate culture to the human resources department. HR managers certainly give it their best shot.

Culture In Theory

Propaganda
- Cherish Customers
- Value Employees
- Open Door Policy
- ...
- ...

Culture In Practice

Reality
- Self-Interests
- Politics
- Individualist
- ...
- ...

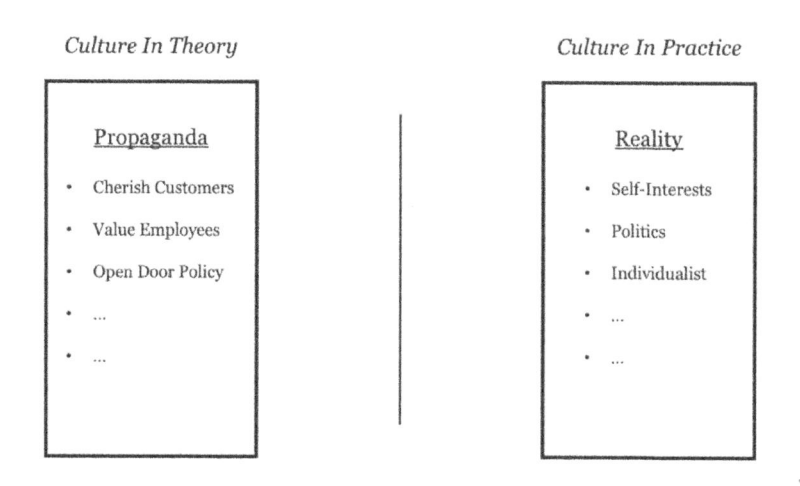

Figure 5: Propaganda Versus Reality

But the emphasis is on culture in theory. They attempt to articulate the desired cultural state via a plethora of media. They create videos and posters. They hang banners and flags. Awards go to employees who best exemplify the desired attributes.

But usually, this is the extent of it, and culture in action takes on a different look. Employees actually behave according to their own, and usually very different, de facto value system. If individual accountability is valued on a daily basis more than teamwork, and if individuals are measured and rewarded, then the culture that arises from those concrete behaviors is an *individualist* culture, not a team culture.

The Focus Is Too Often on Roles

It seems apparent that managers in these firms are more interested in installing systems and processes yielding (hopefully) reliable outcomes than they are in creating ways to live up to their stated values. Like a family indulging in a Saturday evening board game at the dining room table, where parents and kids move their plastic pieces around the cardboard landscape, managers strive to place people in "roles" in which they interact within prescribed boundaries and rules. The human element is largely ignored, short of calling out desired attributes such as "hard worker" and "rock star."

The people in charge appear to understand the challenge broadly as, "How do we get people to behave optimally to the firm's benefit?" The fix, they would argue, is in the exercise of management, best represented by a reporting structure and corporate organization with all the roles, bosses, and operational process money can buy. And certainly, with the emphasis on data, analytics, predictive analytics, and artificial intelligence in the modern business world, it's no wonder that managers pursue methods and measurable practices with such vigor.

People of course, are not robots. They bring to the workplace not only skills but also their biases, needs, and desires, along with their fears, doubts, and dysfunctions. And as they mix, the cocktail rarely maintains any resemblance to the recipe put forth by the bartender. Authentic people, that is to say, "real people," are not synonymous with roles such as "marketing manager" and "sales executive," any more than Julie Andrews should be confused with Mary Poppins.

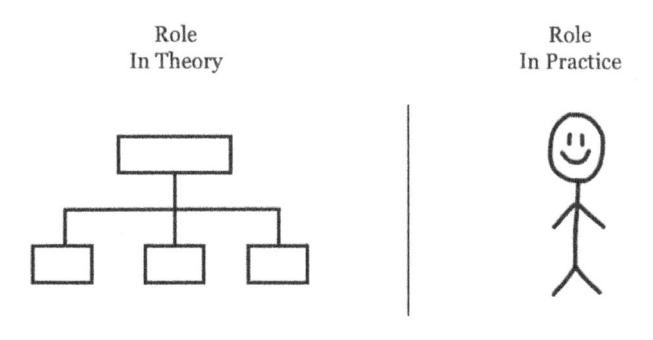

Figure 6: Roles and People

In the case of Andrews, we *know* she is acting when we see her in the movies. Furthermore, *she* knows she is acting, as do all the other people she encounters in positions of cast member, director, producer, key grip, and editor. In business, however, it is not often understood that people are acting in their roles. What is real? What is in character?

Why Change Now?

In a startup, founders behave more authentically. They have to. Their personal attributes, their ideas, their products and services, and their ability to interact with customers are all very connected. CEOs and newly hired staff are consistently passionate about what they are doing. They communicate

27

with each other, as well as with customers, with a sense of urgency, care, and conviction.

Clearly, this is all part of the mythology of startups. I don't mean to suggest that all founders and senior leaders who join a firm early in its life are inherently honorable or exemplary by any ethical standard. Early-stage firms are full of senior leaders who are completely disingenuous about why they are doing what they are doing. They strive to serve the customer not so much for principled reasons but rather to exit as soon as possible, for as much as possible, no matter who gets hurt. But they do, at the end of the day, serve the customer with zeal, regardless of the hidden motivation.

In startups, people generally engage in less role-playing, and behave more authentically, than in later-stage firms. Roles, if adopted at all, tend to be ambiguous and overlapping between staff. "We all wear a lot of hats around here" is a refrain we've all heard from entrepreneurial staff in young firms. To act in a narrow role or take on the prescribed behavior outlined in a job description would be difficult, if not impossible, for an embryonic firm's employees to pull off.

In the norm, early-stage firms enjoy a level of congruence between culture in theory and culture in practice. A firm's survival demands execution of the basic elements of business operations with maximum effort and focus. Little time is available for game playing. Generally, there is a high correlation in startups between who-we-say-we-are and how-we-behave.

Contrast that with larger firms, wherein roles, organization charts, processes, and systems drive the commercial operating machinery. The entire business is built on roles that fulfill their duties in a prescribed manner. It is like a movie or a Broadway play in which the roles (characters) behave within a framework (plot) and are afforded the chance for specific interactions within clear boundaries (script). But unlike a play on the stage, people acting in roles in business do not deliver their lines verbatim. The affair is more like an improvisational performance. They make stuff up.

As employees bring to work their human traits, the cultural schism is nearly unavoidable. Managers in larger firms focus on performance based on the expectations of the role. Staff focus on fulfillment, status, security, and advancement based on their personal desires. In the futile attempt to direct staff as human beings, management tries to articulate a set of desired attributes. They create the posters. They write the employee manuals, guides, and policy that form the visible elements of the espoused culture in theory. Employees then form their own culture in practice, very different from the theory. The tragic result is culture as propaganda.

In a large firm, the cultural dissonance doesn't necessarily negatively affect financial performance. In fact, one could argue to the contrary. Big companies thrive every day, as employees assume roles, perform duties in a nest of processes, and interact with systems while politics carry on in the background. It is all understood and accepted as part of the deal. How else to manage an organization composed of tens of thousands or hundreds of thousands of staff? Managers of large firms may have little choice but to install role-based systems, complete with all the employee acting, and accept the dissonance between culture in theory and culture in practice as the cost of admission.

But for CEOs of smaller firms attempting to grow to mid-size success, they *do* have a choice. Does the leader perpetuate the idea of congruence between culture in theory and culture in practice, as often experienced in the initial stages of a firm's lifespan? Or does the leader succumb to the methods, paradigms, and role-playing on vivid display in larger firms and, in so doing, introduce espoused culture as propaganda, leaving culture in practice to be organically formulated and installed by the staff themselves?

For me, the choice is crystal clear. I pick door No. 1. The CEO can lead a small company to a transformative, financially lucrative outcome as a direct result of ensuring full congruence between culture in theory and culture in practice. It is job No. 1 for the CEO.

People, of course, hold a variety of personal values. For them to join a firm with similar corporate values is easy and ultimately fulfilling. But in the event that people hold different values than the firm, their choice is less clear. Can they sign up to corporate behavioral expectations (e.g. teamwork) even if they hold different values personally (such as I-win-you-lose paradigms)? In other words, can they suspend their personal beliefs and commit, in sincerity, to those of the organization when on company time?

In practice, I have found that differing personal beliefs can be dismissed as long as the right actions, consistent with corporate culture in theory, are exercised. Corporate culture is not the basis for a cult. We do not attempt to win over people's personal value systems. But we do expect people to adopt cultural values in the context of doing their jobs. Congruence between a company's culture in theory and culture in practice is measured by the behavior exhibited by each participant, plain and simple. Behavior, then, ensures compliance.

In Sum

- Many organizations conflate their publicly stated culture with a declared set of values.

- Espoused values, which are "culture in theory," are often different from values or culture in action. What we say about ourselves, and want others to believe about us, can be different from how we behave.

- Culture in theory can be dismissed as propaganda by employees, who behave consistently with their own value systems.

- Managers often attempt to get the most out of their employees by assigning roles.

- Managers too often neglect the dissonance between roles in theory and roles in action, as acted by real people with their own agendas.

- CEOs of growing firms must confront the fundamental challenge of ensuring congruence between culture in theory and culture in practice.

Culture in Practice

In reflecting about the first few months of my time as CEO, consciously formulating the required elements of our culture in action to grow our company to mid-level success demanded a frank analysis of where we were. What was working, and why? What was not working, and why? In our case, we wanted to spend more time looking at the why.

I think it can be too easy for organizations, in the heat of operating, to neglect to look closely at what is working. It can take the form of the mystical: "Don't touch it or you'll break it." And many organizations fail to fully analyze why something isn't working: "Just try something else." In both cases, a deeper understanding of the *why* can be crucial.

In the case of growing our firm, ad hoc and informal processes broadly explained the *what* of things that were working well. We enjoyed customer intimacy and an efficiency in operating.

The *why* question could be addressed in a number of ways. We were disruptors in a vibrant market full of incumbents. Our products had advantages that met well with market trends. But at the end of the day, the most impactful part of our success had to do with our staff and their commitment to each other and to customers.

It was largely taken for granted that many employees behaved with unbridled sincerity and unwavering passion. Nobody told them to act this way. They just did. How, then, to put that spirit in a jar and perpetuate it as new people joined the company at an accelerated pace and the complexity of running the business inevitably grew deeper?

We determined that two cultural attributes would serve as the cornerstones of our desired state: trust and teamwork.

Usually, in everyday life, people tend to offer trust to others based on past experience. In other words, folks are deemed trustworthy as a consequence of deeds or acts already committed. In our case, we wanted to declare a commitment to trust independent of history or bias. Employees and customers would be viewed as trustworthy, period. We would proclaim the overt intention to trust their future acts, deeds, statements, and motivations. And we would be transparent about our intent to trust and be trusted.

Secondly, we would exalt teamwork. And by teamwork, I mean very literally to put the needs, objectives, constraints, incentives, and rewards of the team before any individual. The results of our firm were at stake; it is the team that must excel across all functions and all levels. Division of labor and structural organization would be necessary, certainly, but we wanted to build a company that required our staff to exhibit a higher level of commitment to the team than to self-interest. And we desired deep relationships with customers where they thought of us as one cohesive unit and enjoyed unparalleled levels of service from our firm, top to bottom.

Though perhaps the team concept is not radical in nature, we wanted to push the boundaries of what was possible for a firm to behave as the best teams have performed in history. Think of the teams that put a man on the moon or executed the evacuation from Dunkirk. Or the '69 Miracle Mets or the '93

Chicago Bulls. They all shared a conviction and a commitment with clear expectations for what it would mean to win or lose together. Can one bring that sort of teamwork to the table in business? I sure wanted to try.

Employees would be expected to act as adults, treating one another the way they want to be treated. But in our case, the notion of acting as adults would carry an additional burden for everyone. If you reflect on your own experiences throughout your career, you may agree that many small-company CEOs think of themselves as parents and their employees as children. I wonder if sometimes employees like it this way because it absolves them of responsibility for many things, including independent thought. One can hide, essentially, behind what the CEO puts up for all to follow. If things go wrong, it's not my fault, it's the boss's.

In our case, the adult paradigm would be crucial. The news of the day isn't always rosy. We did not want a culture wherein managers are in one room talking about how to deal with reality, while employees are in other rooms scampering about their business in a vacuum. We wanted to be open with each other, and for each other.

For the values of teamwork and trust to truly take effect, we would further require *our* adults to behave with a much higher sense of responsibility than expected elsewhere. It would not be a matter of where one lived on the org chart that would set our expectation for them behaving thoughtfully. This would mean calling out issues, and the people associated with the issues, outside their immediate purview. Employees would be expected to think and act independently of management-supplied permission slips and treasure the values of teamwork and trust, all while confronting conflict routinely. And if they were asked to do something they felt unqualified to do, the burden would be on *them* to seek the proper coaching. We would trust our employees to get the job done as one team, avoiding an instruction-based orientation in our day-to-day operations.

We would empathize, in the complete sense of that word, with our customers, as together the parties would seek transparent agreements in the best interest of everyone. Honesty and authenticity in character would prevail.

Transparent + Agreement = Transparent Agreement

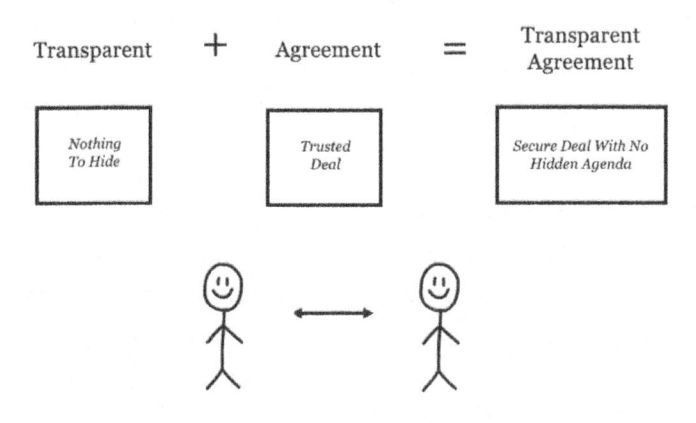

Nothing To Hide | Trusted Deal | Secure Deal With No Hidden Agenda

Figure 7: Transparent Agreement

"Transparent" and "agreement" are two terms all readers understand. But we rarely see them together in the wild. Agreements that are familiar to us tend to be formal and, usually, written. Purchase orders and sales contracts offer the most vivid examples. Two parties agree, in writing, within a legal framework that includes terms for invoicing, payment, cancellation, warranty, indemnity, force majeure, arbitration, litigation, and a host of other issues. Though the writing is legally precise, it is not, most certainly transparent. Legal agreements are, as expressed in the fine print, as much about getting out of a deal as about describing the terms of actually doing the deal.

We wanted to treat our customers in such a way that there was no fine print, conceptually. We would extend the transparent elements of the informal agreements, held in handshake form, over to the formal. Our empathy for the customer would be felt, expressed, and executed as part of these transparent agreements.

Furthermore, if we were to do it right, staff would feel an intrinsic satisfaction in what they were doing and look to remain with our firm through thick and thin. This would create a sense of stability for our organization, and the staff could exhibit a nimbleness to respond thoughtfully as our state of affairs would, of course, continuously evolve.

It was my job as CEO to make sure that the team was focused on the right priorities and that corporate objectives were well understood by everyone. Our company goals had to be intertwined with the way people behaved day-to-day — no small matter. The mission was connecting the dots for everyone so they could comprehend and give care to the corporate agenda as they completed the tasks of their specific roles. Collaboration was not going to be a nice-to-have but rather an axiomatic component of our culture. Outliers would be called out for transgressions and rehabilitated or removed.

Peer-to-Peer Culture, Defined

I wanted to run the company in as straightforward a style as possible. And I would expect the same from staff, communicating in a direct, clear manner at every turn even when conversations were difficult. We would be relentless in our pursuit for success. All our eyes would rest on the same prize.

Peer-to-Peer Culture

Treat Each Other As Peers With An Emphasis on Authenticity

TRUST

TEAM ORIENTATION

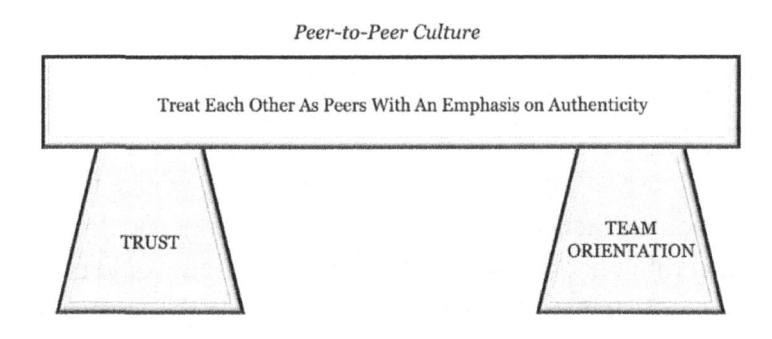

Figure 8: Peer-to-Peer Culture

We called our culture in practice, maintaining these desired attributes, *peer-to-peer culture*. We would treat each other as peers, meaning as equals, with an emphasis on authenticity. Posturing and other forms of corporate role-playing would be taboo. In defining the idea of "treat each other," we were careful to be inclusive of not only employees but also customers. And we would install trust and a team orientation as the two pillars of our foundation.

The benefits we envisioned, and ultimately enjoyed, in our peer-to-peer culture were plentiful, but two stand out. The first is alignment. We saw optimal alignment between our firm's key objectives and the exhibited behavior of personnel. In our model, we implemented a successful scheme in which senior management interpreted the needs of owners, customers, and employees, and put forth the corporate goals each year. Employees shared in cross-functional initiatives and were paid as a team based on the overall success of these initiatives, rather than on individual success more commonly found in OKR models. Peer-to-peer did not mean democracy. Goals were communicated top-down. But these goals, along with their associated set of corporate initiatives, served as the backbone for explicit team-based employee behavior that held its reward in a team-based pay plan.

Success, as measured by the achievement of goals, is not guaranteed. But a company puts itself in a great position for success if all the staff are aligned. Whether it be revenue, gross margin, market share, return on equity, or any other of the metrics at stake, the staff must behave collectively to achieve the goals. Provided that goals are achievable, an aligned organization has a far greater probability of success.

We also wanted the staff to feel an intrinsic satisfaction. Self-confidence, self-esteem, and a recognition of company spirit are infectious, rolling up to high morale in the aggregate. In a trusted culture, people feel trustworthy. When direct, honest communication is the standard, people feel like they can be honest and direct. It is irresistible. People have fun in their jobs and increase their commitment to the firm's interests.

Commitment of this magnitude motivates people to proactively balance personal life and professional life, willingly checking email in the evening from home after they enjoyed time during the afternoon to tend to a child's needs. It is a fluid trade between company needs and employee needs, rather than a time-based, punch-in, punch-out model. Some pundits would argue this fluid effect is "unhealthy," and people are better served when there is a clear line between work and personal time. I could not disagree with those critics more emphatically. Experience tells me that when employees gain intrinsic satisfaction from their commitment, and burdens are shared fairly between teammates and company, the model works reliably. A labor of love prevails for all.

Actually Doing It

To actually put it all in practice, though, I had to own it. Personally. Yes, I was a peer among peers. But to put it all into practice, I was the role model. I alone could evangelize the essence of peer-to-peer culture without any fear of getting it wrong. As people watched and listened, they mimicked the behavior.

I think it is imperative that a CEO or other, unambiguous leader of an organization assume the role of "chief culture officer." I am not suggesting a literal assignment of the culture title to the CEO, as contrived titles do nothing but prop up appearances and reinforce culture-as-propaganda. But rather, the CEO has to be the one who declares the peer-to-peer culture and defines the core elements. Every speech and every email must exude the essence of desired cultural elements.

Let's face it: Most firms have problems all over the place, ranging from function to function, and affecting all parts of the organization. That was undeniably true in our case. The challenge is how to unlock insights from the people closest to the action, as they usually have the best information about cause, implications, and potential resolution of issues they encounter day-to-day. Factory floors that employ those doing the work of manufacturing offer a good example. Line workers routinely understand best when quality becomes compromised, and they're able to diagnose breakdowns in process and loopholes in quality control. Gaining access to their perspective is essential. But a backdrop of trust is mandatory. Within a culture of trust, people with insights communicate more fully, more honestly, and more often.

Vulnerability plays a huge part in peer-to-peer culture. Senior leaders must expose their own weaknesses, particularly when dealing with internal issues with staff. How else can we expect the working team to openly discuss issues without fear, conscious or not, of retribution, embarrassment, and harm to reputation? The questions to ask, brainstorm, and resolve must be rendered in a safe, trusted business landscape. If I, as the CEO, am comfortable exposing a lack of understanding and an inability to propose a specific solution and am self-aware of my limitations in the way that I engage with staff, then they can respond in kind. We will get the best outcomes when we focus on what is broken, and what must be done differently, without the posturing, one-upmanship, and political maneuvering all too common in many companies.

In peer-to-peer culture, a weakness, is not a negative attribute. "I don't know how" is a perfectly safe thing to say.

There are plenty of people to help. To pretend to know how to do something, and affect team goals, however, is anathema. The usual triggers for one's corporate ego are flipped upside down in peer-to-peer. It is compliance with culture, and a persistent desire to get better and do better as a teammate, that matters.

I believe that if a CEO declares trust and teamwork as the cornerstones of a desired peer-to-peer culture, and constantly reinforces the declaration in the daily affairs in the workplace, the chances of successful implementation of culture are very high. The declaration is a necessary part of the quest — though not the only part. The culture must be implemented consistently in policy and day-to-day operations. The culture is installed, every day, in a hundred different ways. It's a job that is never done. One missed opportunity, one false note, and a lot of good work can be undone.

Management must be the stewards for ongoing execution according to the cultural principles. In fact, the management team as a whole plays a crucial role in successful installation of peer-to-peer culture with the rank and file. Yes, the CEO sets the clear standard as role model in chief. But other senior management have the essential duty to behave with consistency and manage frontline staff day-to-day.

To Be Accountable

Interestingly, accountability is a valued component in a peer-to-peer culture, though in a very different context than usual. Typically, the notion of accountability is directly tied to an individual with respect to a set of expectations, commonly made explicit through something like an OKR system.

The good news is roles are made clear through these kinds of systems. What exactly am I supposed to be working on, and to what end? Look no further than to my OKRs to find out. Employees may have external customers to which they must attend. Or perhaps they deliver products and services to internal customers. The point is one of emphasis. The employee is accountable at a task level to deliver whatever they are supposed to deliver, to whoever their customer is, in order to keep the machine running.

The bad news is that individual accountability, as tied to systems such as OKRs, is also a prelude to reward or punishment *as individuals*. Thus, staff tend to behave with an emphasis on their self-interests in order to maximize the rewards and minimize the punishments. They self-promote and posture. They suck up to management. They engage in games whereby winners (us) and losers (them) materialize. Politics are followed by more politics. And virtually all of it is *not* in the best interests of the firm.

In a peer-to-peer culture, accountability is based on adherence to the culture itself. This statement is simple enough. But it may be the most counterintuitive, yet powerful, notion of peer-to-peer culture.

In our model of organizational behavior, accountability at a task level is subordinate to accountability at the level of cultural attribute. In practice, this means that employees know beyond any doubt that adherence to the cultural standard is mandatory. If someone behaves outside the standard, they are accountable for their actions. Repercussions up to and including termination of employment are at stake. It is not

43

good enough to say "I did my job" if the culture is threatened by that employee's actions or deeds.

Peer-to-Peer Accountability

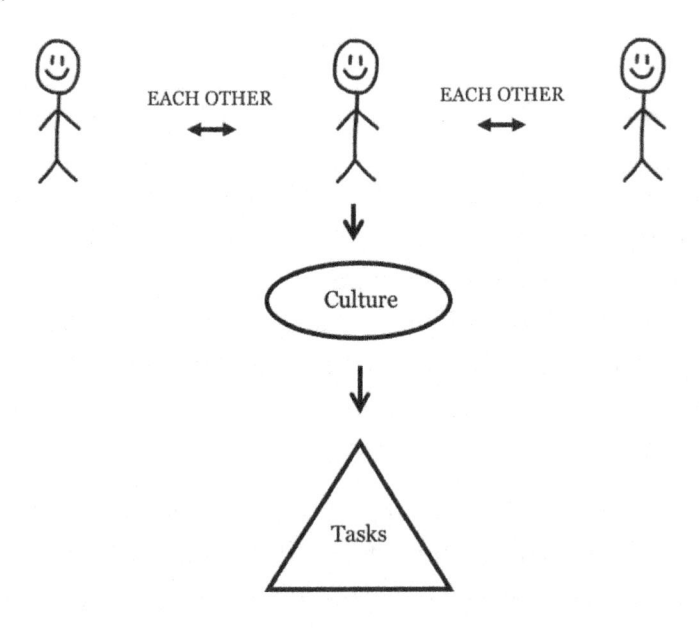

Figure 9: Peer-to-Peer Accountability

You may be wondering how far I am suggesting we go with this concept in practical terms. Am I literally saying that employees can flub every task they are given, but if they are culturally aligned, they are OK? Not quite.

In peer-to-peer culture, we still require competency. Employees must be hired according to standards of aptitude and experience, and managed to a set of task-level expectations. But, if an employee is having a difficult time performing their duties, the whole company is conditioned and incentivized to work with that individual to grow their competency to the minimum standard within a prescribed time frame. If the employee still cannot meet the minimum standard, they are told so and are terminated.

But competency, in and of itself, is not enough to maintain one's employment. The converse case, in which the star employee is noncompliant with the culture, is perversely easier to remedy. Noncompliant stars are rehabilitated or removed. Period. Individual performers are not held to a different standard because of their task-level contribution. It can be painful to administer, for sure, with material effects on the business. But it has to be done.

During my three-year run as CEO, in which we employed about 120 people, we had about six or seven employees that we had to fire because of noncompliance with our peer-to-peer culture. In one case, it was a breach in teamwork. A sales manager incessantly argued about her "territory," and credit due for transient success, while lacking the will to help others in need. In another case, a product developer would not engage in open, trusted dialogue about features and future roadmap. The person sought back-channel, hidden forums to "sneak in" features that were not overtly agreed upon. In each case, employees were asked to reform and comply. When they didn't, they were terminated.

But, during the same three-year period, we only had to let one employee go for performance reasons related to competency. We hired him, in hindsight, with aptitude that was insufficient to do the job effectively. It was our fault as much as his, but we had hoped that along the way he would learn, grow, and become competent. He didn't or couldn't. It was a real shame, because the individual was a stellar member of the team with respect to cultural compliance. We tried and tried to fix the task-level issues, but ultimately, we had to move to termination for everyone's well-being.

Yes, All the Fuss Is About Culture

It can sound fanatical to leaders in companies today, priding themselves on best-in-class management doctrine, to place such an emphasis on culture. But that is indeed what I am saying. When people stray, they must be corrected or removed from the organization. With such an emphasis on the attribute of trust in peer-to-peer cultures, employees, customers and third parties must be able to "trust the trust." In other words, if the CEO says that trust is a top cultural attribute, then people must experience this trust when things go bad or when someone misbehaves.

Deeds considered untrustworthy cannot be accepted as permissible. These deeds include, at a minimum, throwing colleagues under the bus, deflecting work to others out of laziness or fear, posturing about one's contributions as special or elite, and incessant vague language to communicate one's mistakes.

To maintain a culture of trust-the-trust, we must be ruthless in our installment. Expressions such as, "Put your money where your mouth is," or, "Don't just talk the talk, walk the walk" come to mind. Cultural values will always be tested in a peer-to-peer culture. The important consideration is how management behaves when outlier behaviors surface. Is the culture protected or compromised in the face of stress? CEOs must be prepared to answer the question decisively and act.

For me, reflecting on my time as CEO, the action took the following form:

1. Declare behavioral expectations.

We explicitly declared our key cultural attributes of teamwork and trust at every opportunity, right from the first meeting with a potential new hire or a customer. It was explicit. We said who we were, then behaved consistently with what we said.

2. Hold staff to those expectations.

Holding staff to behave consistently with expectations for cultural compliance was straightforward, as we relied on the age-old principle of peer-level management. Nobody wanted to let anybody else down. When they did, peers blew the whistle. Peer-to-peer culture enabled peers to hold each other to account. It was peer pressure, shining like a beacon. Management was sometimes the last to know if an employee was misbehaving relative to notions of trust or teamwork. In essence, the whole affair was self-policing. Management was there for escalation, rather than spying.

3. Correct behavior.

Guilty parties were given a chance for rehab. It was a public event. Many employees contributed to the cause via informal conversation and group meetings wherein we confronted the person. It was a sign of deep care. We wanted the person to comply and offered all the perspective we could. We recognized, for example, that other parts of life can motivate self-interest over teamwork (such as a mortgage payment). People worry about security, status, and survival. We had to deal with these very real fears by explaining how everyone wins, without exception, if the team wins based on a paradigm emphasizing trust. Some got it quickly. Some resisted before comprehending. We tried to assure all staff that their personal values were acknowledged. But holding a commitment to company goals and achieving them, in the way we prescribed, was held as necessary for employment.

4. Expel the outliers.

When outliers would not, or could not, conform to our cultural expectations despite multiple attempts at rehab we fired them. The action was always humane, as best we could make it, relative to severance and other details. It was not necessarily the employee's "fault" that cultural compliance was elusive. But we always acted swiftly. It was not fair to everyone else if we let someone wreck a good thing. I never regretted acting swiftly.

Having the right team members was critically important. Candidates were recruited to join the company not only because of their skills and experience but also from a profile that maximized the chances of their own success as contributing members of a peer-to-peer culture. Getting the right people in the org chart, as defined by cultural compliance, is as important as getting the most-skilled candidates. I will have more to say about that later, in the chapter about hiring.

Once we assembled the core team of committed personnel, who bought into our culture completely, the rest of our challenges seemed less daunting. Competitive firms posed obstacles, certainly, as they offered products that were sometimes better, and sometimes cheaper, depending on the customer's needs and wants. Market conditions ebbed and flowed, requiring nimble responsiveness. And the overall challenge of executing across the functional disciplines of sales, marketing, administration, help desk, and product development never left us bored.

But the culture carried the day.

In Sum

- The culture in practice that we wanted is grounded in trust and teamwork. We call it peer-to-peer culture.

- Benefits of peer-to-peer culture include alignment of corporate goals to team performance and great commitment from the intrinsically satisfied staff.

- Accountability in peer-to-peer culture is to each other and to the culture. Accountability to task-level achievements is subordinate to those.

- Ability to acknowledge weakness is a prized attribute in the culture. "I don't know how" or "I don't understand" are welcome sentiments.

- Team performance, not individual performance is incentivized and rewarded.

- Posturing, lazy behavior, and vague explanations for mistakes are anathema.

- A climate of trust-the-trust must be installed. Compliance is mandatory. Outliers are rehabilitated or removed, regardless of task-level competency.

The 5 Attributes of Peer-to-Peer Culture

Trust

Team Orientation

Empathy

Honesty

Dynamic Action

Trust

The evolution of technology that people have enjoyed in their personal lives has also forever changed the mindset of work. Mobile phones and laptops provide tool-anywhere opportunity. Applications such as Skype and Slack offer the chance to use these tools for collaboration, among other things. Employees want the freedom to work from home, at least some of the time. And, popular culture has changed over the last 50 years. We expect both parents to share in child-raising, child-minding, and child-transporting, regardless of earning power.

Furthermore, in many metropolitan areas where people live, the sheer number of cars on the road presents outrageous commuting challenges. Employees argue that their productivity is higher on the days when they work from home. They will inevitably spend time that otherwise would be wasted commuting on work.

So, the battle is on. Trust, or the lack thereof, is at stake. Does the firm trust employees to manage their own schedules and work from wherever they want? Or do senior management act on the prejudice that people, if given the opportunity, loaf or pursue personal priorities? The perception of human nature, and the need to control it, can exacerbate fears and anxieties with shareholders who watch from afar and board members who are caught in the middle. Senior management, then, must invent policy to form the basis for trust, and, through compliance, create the evidence to be trustworthy.

Trust in the abstract is a simple concept, though it carries a couple of variants, depending on the context. The Merriam-Webster dictionary offers two definitions, the first of which is: *"assured reliance on the character, ability, strength, or truth of someone or something; one in which confidence is placed."*[6] I think the key word is "confidence." This definition stops short of implying a guarantee, but confidence connotes something strong, very much on the continuum toward a guarantee. When we trust someone, we are confident that attributes of integrity, sincerity, and truth will prevail.

Personally, I adore this definition and think it applies well to our business setting. In practice, to trust someone requires a leap of faith. It requires the one offering trust to be vulnerable to the possibility of disappointment or betrayal. Words are not simply received as benign. There is an accompanying implied promise. Trusted communication tenders a gravity of take-it-to-the-bank.

Contrast that to the concept of distrust, where we have no confidence whatsoever that the other party will act from these attributes. We don't know what to expect from a person we distrust, but we certainly don't expect a successful outcome based on truth and sincere intent.

A second definition Merriam-Webster puts forth is also very suitable to describe trust in the sense of business and human relationships: *"care, such as the custody of a child committed to her trust; a charge or duty imposed in faith or confidence or as a condition of some relationship, or something*

---

[6] https://www.merriam-webster.com/dictionary/trust

committed or entrusted to one to be used or cared for in the interest of another. "Imagine working with a set of people who hold themselves to the standard of child caretaker. That is, a standard that expects people to show care for the concepts and ideas of others. It rings a tone of unselfishness.

Trust, then, is about confidence and care. We place confidence in people to develop their thoughts and attend to their chores with care.

It all sounds very Pollyanna, some might argue. No, I am not suggesting an untenable utopian state. In my experience, creating a corporate culture anchored in trust, whereby people routinely communicate in a direct, honest manner, is possible. It is an act of will. Trusted cultures don't "just happen" as arbitrary phenomena. They must be consciously created and actively nurtured.

In Peer-to-Peer, Trust Is Declared, Not Earned

As the concept of trust applies directly to peer-to-peer culture, it is a matter of proactive confidence in staff, partners, and customers, in an environment where all people exercise care unilaterally. Peer-to-peer culture requires an initial leap of faith from all participants as the price of entry. Everyone must agree to rely on the word of others, taken at face value. Collectively, it is a state of communal, assured reliance.

In peer-to-peer culture, there is no rite of passage whereby someone *becomes* trustworthy. Nothing is earned. There is no behavioral, historical prerequisite. It is a matter of declaration. We *will* trust and behave in a trustworthy manner. If folks don't comply, they are rehabilitated or removed. In the case of staff, removal means termination. With partners and customers, removal means attrition and cancellation of contracts in an appropriate way.

If people value the concept of trust generally, then why are so many business cultures lacking in trust, enabling rumor and conspiracy to flourish? Think about it. We demand trust in other areas of our lives. Nobody just leaves their 6-month-old baby with any random babysitter. The caretaker must be trusted, explicitly. Trust is an axiom of the contract.

At the office, it is different. Most employees' work experiences are centered around moments when, according to their own narratives, they acted in good faith and others did not. Most acutely, they then suffered the consequences. Over time, mistrust becomes the prevailing attitude. It only takes a few cases of demonstrated untrustworthy behavior people to develop a personal philosophy that the workplace should not be trusted. Best to be on your guard at all times.

Overzealous attempts to control employee behavior don't help. In cases in which owners, boards, and by extension senior management act from a base of mistrust, company policy can be overly prescriptive. Inadvertently, the policy can be perceived by employees as downright inflammatory. A we/they paradigm ensues. *They* need strict policy for the number of sick days granted, so *we* don't take too much time off. The we/they phenomenon is further exacerbated as policies proliferate to manage expense reimbursement, purchasing signature authority, and activity reporting.

Yes, owners, boards, and senior management must protect the integrity of the firm from theft and other forms of mischief. Don't get me wrong. Locks, passwords, and other forms of security are good things. But it doesn't take too long for a firm to get carried away with implementation of policy and process that screams, "We don't trust our people."

Game Theory

People aren't stupid. Game theorists have for decades analyzed human behavior in the spirit of one-upmanship. For every rule, there lies a workaround. And, in anticipating the next workaround, management evolves policy and process. The next set of workarounds unfold, and on and on we go. Policy statements become more rigorous, while process improvements yield to complexity.

This is the nature of rule-based systems. We see it routinely in educational institutions, the stock market, digital copyright protection, and countless other places. If one's behavior achieves a desired outcome, regardless of the unintended consequences, it will be indulged in. If the rules do not exclude a behavior, the behavior is permissible. New rules must be written to exclude the heretofore unregulated, undesirable behavior. And new behaviors appear. And new rules are written.

At the office, the more a policy or prescriptive process attempts to restrict employee behavior, the more people look to work around the constraints. They fib. They hide. They are vague in their communication. The rules set by policy, intended to minimize and police bad behavior, render the opposite behavior in staff. The system itself manufactures these symptoms. It is rendered even worse with the increasing friction between an older, conservative, and perhaps antiquated style of company and the new ways of living in the present day.

The realities of employees' personal lives, overlaid with self-interests in status, security, and staying out of trouble, demand their attention to priorities that are likely to exacerbate their noncompliance with corporate policy. People are prone to manufacture sick days and other nonsense to create space for themselves to manage their priorities, as a simple example. They sneak out of the office early, hoping not to be noticed, in order to catch the 4 p.m. track meet in which a family member is participating. Wouldn't be better if employees were simply trusted?

Certainly, policy in a corporate setting is required to a minimum standard. A company is a legal entity doing business, to one degree of another, in markets under the rule of law and regulatory control. Additional levels are required if data is held on individuals, among other reasons. In other words, not all policy and procedure is voluntary or discretionary. And not all of the policy and procedure that's voluntary is put in place to discipline employees.

Corporate risk mitigation policy, as we know, focuses on issues such as potential litigation and legal trouble. Policy takes the form of insurance, essentially, against the legal risk. And it is the insurance that drives compliance. It is important, for example, to maintain policy about discrimination and sexual harassment.

In this way, boards can protect companies from outlier behavior, whereby an employee may behave poorly. It is important to say clearly, "We do not condone the behavior of

Chris. We maintain policy that all employees are aware of, and we take these matters very seriously." So, there you go. Chris is in trouble, which is as it should be. But the firm carries on. Policy protects the firm's interests.

Similarly, corporate process is necessary so that the company can operate effectively. How to pay people, invoice customers, test products, and maintain a website? These are all activities that are best served with reliable, repeatable process. The slippery slope, however, emerges in how these processes evolve in practice. Does the designer of the process assume trust or mistrust as the central theme?

In truth, some policies and processes have a greater effect on corporate culture than others. But in too many cases, a line is crossed, and the dominant motivations are no longer attainment of corporate objectives and reasonable mitigation of risk. Employees are asked to follow rules and adhere to processes that go well beyond a rational foundation of corporate compliance in the legal and regulatory sense. And in that circumstance, people inevitably and unapologetically game the system and find their own path.

Case in Point: Should We Let Them Work From Home?

Consider the policy decision many organizations face concerning the work-from-home question. Many companies have good reason to insist their employees do their work in the office. Healthcare and manufacturing jobs are good examples. It's hard to catch a fish if the fisherman doesn't show up to the pond. But many, many firms are challenged to allow their employees the permission to work from home. What started as "casual Friday" is now being considered "work from home Friday." The structure offered by the bricks and mortar location become tested when people begin to manage to their own schedules and are less visible to the boss.

In this debate, the firm's objectives are to ensure maximum performance from the staff. Occasionally, an employee's role is independent and can be executed in a near vacuum from others. But usually, collaboration among organizational members and between organizations is a must for a successful outcome. The marketing team must work together, sharing ideas and debating tactics. And marketing must work with technical staff, sales, and other functional organizations to ensure the successful flow of ideas, programs, and developments across the company. Isn't all this done best with everyone in attendance in the office?

The pandemic of 2020 has obviously had a massive impact on the debate, as firms are literally forced to engage in work-from-home models as routine. Many like it. Brianne Kimmel, a venture capitalist and founder of Work Life Ventures, wrote an opinion piece for The Guardian titled *The Office Is Obsolete. And That's a Good Thing.* She goes so far as to say, "A world where the office is obsolete is more positive, more communal, and more productive."[7]

Some managers are even finding, in so many words, "Wow, we actually *can* trust our employees to work from home." But this sentiment does not yet appear to be the norm. There are still plenty of managers retaining their assumption that employees are not to be trusted. It's just that now the rules

---

[7] https://www.theguardian.com/commentisfree/2020/may/26/the-office-covid-coronavirus-obsolete

have changed. In these scenarios, employees' time at their desk is monitored, cameras must be turned on, and dress must meet a minimum standard of "looking professional." What will be the long-term, new-normal equilibrium on this issue? We shall see.

The Dilemma of Trust

Without question, people value the quality of trust a great deal in their personal lives. We trust our husbands and wives. We trust our closest friends. We trust the motorists on the other side of the yellow line to obey the rules of the road and not crash head-on into us as we pass with mere feet between our cars.

And generally, we trust ourselves. In fact, when others declare they don't trust us, we take it personally. How dare you call me untrustworthy? Most of us prize feeling trustworthy, which drives integrity, fairness, and a sense of well-being.

What a shame, then, that a person who has the inclination to trust must go to work every day in an environment based on lack of trust. The consequence, in the worst case, is they decommit from work. Clearly, a trust-based workplace should be psychologically beneficial for an employee and should motivate commitment.

The crux of the dilemma is we are conditioned to trust based on acts and deeds experienced in the past. We trust based on history. We trust our spouses because we have come to know them, cherish them, and, to a large extent, predict their future behavior. Same goes for close friends. And, in the motorist example, history tells us from thousands and perhaps millions of discrete events, wherein other cars do, in fact, stay on their side of the road as we pass, that we can trust future events in kind.

But outside of known and observed relationships, trusting is riskier. And it doesn't help that we are told, explicitly, to watch out for ourselves by authority figures.

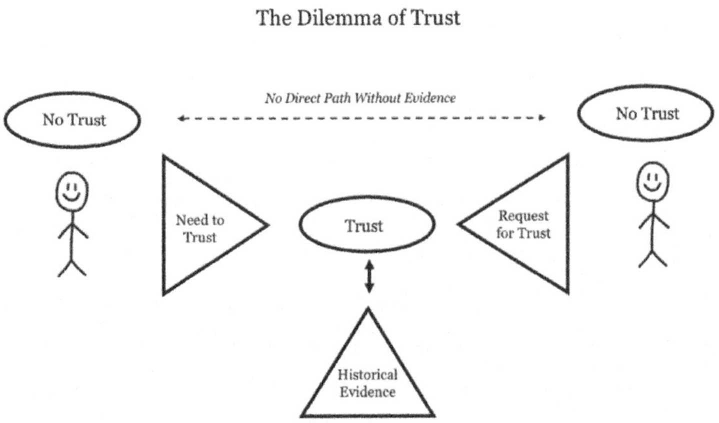

The Dilemma of Trust

Figure 10: The Dilemma of Trust

Parents tell us not to talk to strangers, and governments tell us not to travel to "dangerous" parts of the world. When we trust and are burned by it — whether by a friend, family member, colleague, or a stranger — it feels terrible. One has a feeling of being violated. And the bystanders don't help, as those watching our mistakes mock us for being foolish, stupid, and naive. We learn to be less trusting in future encounters.

Mistrust Finds a Home at the Office

The very nature of organizing a company's human resources can promote mistrust. Our position in the organizational chart demands loyalty to our group, defined as department, functional classification, or geographical designation (e.g. Eastern region or New Jersey office). We attend meetings together and run into each other at the water cooler.

Over time, the human need for socialization kicks in. Conversations stray into rumor and gossip. An "us versus them" dynamic emerges. If left to fester, rumors grow into convenient theories that label others as rivals who maintain agendas that are self-serving rather than in the best interest of the firm. If only *our* department was in charge and *they* got out of the way, then surely *we* would all be better off. In any event, *they* are not to be trusted.

Sometimes the us-versus-them abstraction takes the form of a rebellion against management. It is certainly not uncommon to find a corporate culture whereby the worker layer of the organization chart has no love for the management layer. Cries of incompetence and negligence ring out. These managers don't know what they are doing!

Laurence Peter became famous in 1969 when research led him to the conclusion that people in a hierarchical organization eventually are promoted past their highest level of competence into a position of incompetence. In other words, people rise to their level of incompetence: the Peter Principle[8].

---

[8] Laurence J. Peter and Raymond Hull, *The Peter Principle: Why Things Always Go Wrong* (William Morrow and Company, 1969)

Certainly, we have ample examples of the Peter Principle in action throughout today's business world. One doesn't have to look too hard. In my experience, I've seen it with perfectly competent software developers promoted to first line manager, team lead, and architect, all to a failure. And I've lived it in companies in which high-flying salespeople are promoted to regional managers, only to discover that the skills required for success in that role are different and elusive. And as these incompetent managers exhibit their limitations, subordinates label them as not to be trusted. And so the cycle goes.

Imagine a culture in which people trust each other proactively, essentially aborting the step that requires historical evidence to meet the minimum standard of trustworthiness. It is more like a baby trusting its mother, or a person in distress trusting the EMT, firefighters, and ambulance crew. What if we trusted because we wanted to, as a matter of assertion? What if we *had* to trust?

Peter, I dare say, is on the run in a peer-to-peer organization in which we routinely and reliably trust each other. Should someone be placed into a role that overtaxes their skills or aptitude, others in the organization must rely on the culture as a safe backstop and call out the problem. Incompetence is sniffed out by colleagues, subordinates, and superiors in its early stages. Part of the paradigm of trust is recognition of intents as distinct from outcomes. In other words, in the event someone is placed or promoted over their head, we assume the matter as a mistake and pursue a strategy for resolution. We neither reward nor tolerate sustained incompetence in a company culture anchored in trust.

The Choice for Trust

In peer-to-peer culture, trust is a value, demonstrated by behavior, that we take up by choice. It is an assertion. We will trust. Period. We will behave in a trustworthy manner. Period. The leader makes the declaration and sets the example. Others listen, watch, and follow suit.

In practice, though, installment requires more than merely formulating a declaration and exhibiting the right behavior for others to emulate.

To install trust in a corporate culture, there are obstacles to overcome. The history of distrust, shared by all the people we want to hire, has to be addressed. People's mindsets must be reset before being asked to take the leap of faith that we require. How, then, do we confront the obstacles, achieve this "rewiring," and install trust in the culture?

First, by acknowledging the reality of the employees' experience before enrollment in a peer-to-peer culture. We talk about it, beginning with the first interview with a job candidate. It can be hard for people new to peer-to-peer culture to admit they harbor bad feelings, prejudice, and preconceptions about mistrust in the workplace. Indeed, they are part of the problem, as willing participants in cultures of mistrust, though not with ill intent. It is a coping mechanism in the pursuit of survival. Before people can willingly join a peer-to-peer organization, they must acknowledge the prejudice and come to grips with the powerful history that has formed the bad feelings. Like other forms of rehab, admission is the first step to recovery.

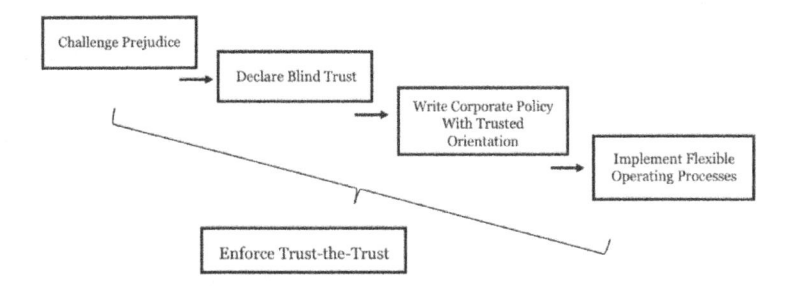

```
Challenge Prejudice
    → Declare Blind Trust
        → Write Corporate Policy
          With Trusted Orientation
            → Implement Flexible
              Operating Processes
    Enforce Trust-the-Trust
```

Figure 11: How to Install Trust

Second, we assert the installment of trust as an axiomatic, unwavering component of peer-to-peer culture. The message is simple. We trust blindly, with no implied correlation to reason, prerequisite, or qualification based on history. We don't wait for a person to earn trust. We just give it to them, straight away. And we are not kidding around. Trust as installed is actionable, observable, and enforceable.

Third, we write corporate policy in such a way that trust is explicitly communicated. We must obliterate the we/they paradigm in form and content. Policy must be written for the collective "us." A policy of, "We use our own judgment and do the right thing" prevails over, for example, "If the office equipment you want to buy exceeds your signature authority by $10 or more, you must get approval from the regional vice president." Or consider how we would consciously implement flexible expense reimbursement policy, for example, as: "We aim to keep our travel costs within budget, while also respecting the challenges our employees experience when they are on the road. We trust our employees to make the best decisions they can and do the right thing as they see it."

Fourth, we ask employees to engage in their work with proactive thought and deed. We specifically write operating process to provide as much on-the-ground decision-making and customization as possible. Employees are taught and asked to think on their feet as participants in process. As long as the working relationship *between* parties is understood, employees have flexibility to interpret circumstances, make decisions, and install custom adaptations to the process at hand. Not surprisingly, new employees find the notion as frightening as it is invigorating. New staff must be encouraged, nurtured, and rewarded with positive feedback often, as they embark on the journey as a trusted member of the staff. Again, saying things like, "I don't know how" or "I don't understand" are perfectly acceptable forms of communication as the employee develops competency.

Fifth, management must ensure that trust can, in and of itself, be trusted. Those who can't or won't comply are removed. The benefit, clearly, is for everyone else. The group prevails. The culture is protected.

It was a curious phenomenon to witness as we grew our firm during my tenure. Skeptics could easily argue that the forces of society, experienced by people in the past as well as the present, would prohibit this sense of "blind" trust we were asking for in the workplace.

Peer-to-Peer Circle of Trust

```
         Behave as
         Trustworthy

Trust-the-Trust        Trust
                       Others
```

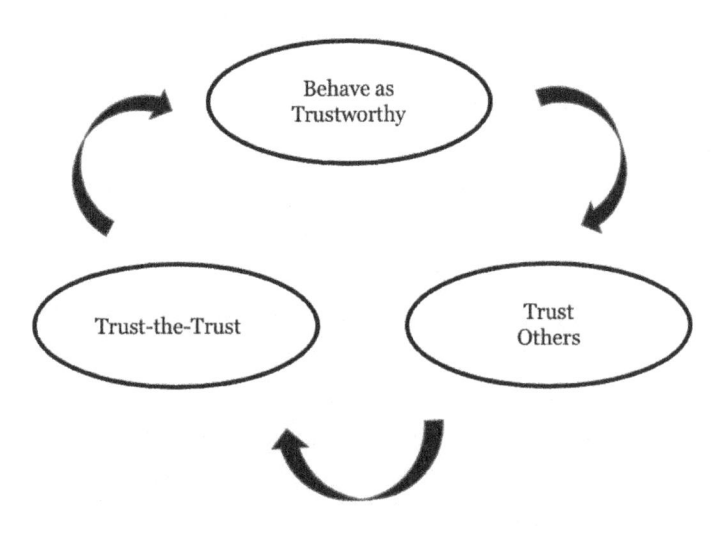

Figure 12: The Circle of Trust

But I found the opposite to be true. Employees were so starved for the quality of trust to emerge, and thirsty to practice deeds based on a trusted environment, that they leaped into our peer-to-peer culture without hesitation and with great enthusiasm. They, in fact, were quick to "trust the trust." And when they experienced the benefits from the culture, in the form of unparalleled intrinsic satisfaction and the spirit of winning together, their enthusiasm grew to unimaginable heights.

The circle of trust, then, relies on behavior and compliance. We ask people to behave in a trustworthy fashion.

We ask for blind trust in others. We form policy and operating processes around trust. And we back it up by enforcing compliance, thus creating a trust-the-trust backbone.

The Burden of Trust

In peer-to-peer culture, the day-to-day personal tugs of doctors' appointments and track meets are all discussed out in the open. There's no hiding or sneaking around. Human nature is such that, if restrained or inhibited, people find ways to seek relief. But if trusted, people feel the burden that comes with being trusted. They behave responsibly.

I find this fact to be as compelling as it is inspiring. When people are decent, committed, and truly trust the trust, they embrace a relentless drive to behave with disproportionately high levels of responsibility as compared to what's seen in typical corporate environments. They do not want to let their peers down. It is only in the rare case, wherein we find people who are not by nature decent or otherwise invested in the trusted culture, that this drive is missing. Thus, the emphasis endures to root out outliers as a condition of success.

When we stop relying on policies and procedures as the primary way to motivate behavior and instead build a culture of trust, people behave in trustworthy ways. Trust, in other words, induces obligation. Anyone frosty enough to boast at the coffee pot about how they are taking excess pleasures from the travel budget is shunned, scolded, and put back in their place. Similarly, middle managers in a peer-to-peer culture, when confronted with a purchasing decision outstripping their signature authority, abstain from gamesmanship to split the purchase into two compliant pieces of lesser amounts and obfuscate the transaction. The culture simply does not accept bad behavior, as peers manage each other.

The idea that peers manage each other is powerful as it is infectious. A CEO can't singularly implore or order people into a cultural norm. It takes a village. But once people subscribe to the value system, and commit themselves as willing participants, noncompliant behavior can't hide. Peers are wholly capable to call out peers for resolution or escalation. And since everybody knows that, everyone feels the tug to comply, willingly and with enthusiasm.

Trust in the workplace does not, however, ensure flawless execution, or somehow create a mistake-free environment. In most business environments, sheer complexity spawns a whole heap of errors. Stuff goes wrong all the time. The key issue, of course, is one of intent.

Take the case whereby Amit makes a mistake that affects Jose in the workplace. Perhaps Amit misunderstood what Jose wanted and delivered the wrong thing. Or maybe Amit was late in delivery for reasons out of his control. Or maybe he just had a brain cramp, plain and simple. Regardless, Jose now experiences the effect of the mistake, and feels anxiety, or perhaps concern for his job, or even anger.

If their relationship is grounded in trust, then they are free to brainstorm a way forward and to discover the cause for the mistake so as to avoid it in the future. But it's not as simple as Amit and Jose defining mutual trust in a corporate culture. Amit's manager must trust Amit. And Jose's manager must trust Jose. Trust must ripple through all the relevant parties in the line of fire for the mistake. This is why compliance, by all parties, is so important. Trust, in other words, is brittle as it is precious.

Nothing poses a threat to a trusted corporate culture quite like the reality of things going wrong. The more things go wrong, the harder it gets to sustain trust. Contemplate a scenario where a firm's revenue is in decline or a competitor enters the market with a hot, new shiny object. Execution in the face of these challenges is the defining moment for management. It is the firms who sustain trust as a core cultural element in these circumstances that triumph.

In the three years I was a CEO, it was never a cakewalk to sustain trust in our culture. We had to work at it. Every day. Societal triggers and misunderstandings were a constant nuisance. But we held firm. We communicated with each other with candor, respect, and care. We valued trust more than any other cultural attribute. We just had to fight off the demons as they appeared.

In the end, the emphasis on maintaining a trusted culture as a corporate axiom must be unrelenting. Peer-to-peer culture relies, fundamentally, on trust to function.

In Sum

- Trust is about confidence and care. We place confidence in people to develop their thoughts and attend to their chores with care.

- In peer-to-peer culture, trust is declared, not earned.

- People are not stupid. They know how to game the system when facing overzealous corporate policy and restrictive operating processes.

- In peer-to-peer, we install trust by:
  - Asking employees to acknowledge their history, prejudices, and mistrust of the workplace.
  - Asserting the expectation for blind trust.
  - Writing corporate policy to minimum standards with an "us" paradigm.
  - Installing operating processes with flexibility and an expectation for thoughtful, organic implementation.
  - Enforcing trust-the-trust via confrontation followed by rehab or removal.

- Trust carries a burden, regulated by peer-level management.

Team Orientation

In a typical corporation, managers look to create space for refuge in the face of trouble. Whatever the problem at hand, it can't be "our fault." Consider the all-too-real example where a firm's revenue is not meeting expectations. A financial plan may call for 35% growth, yet nine months into the year, sales are flat. The marketing VP blames the sale department. "The lead flow was ample," she boasts. "It was the sales team who underperformed, make no mistake about it." "No," says the chief revenue officer, "the problem wasn't with us. It was with product development. They completely screwed up the release of the new product. We've wasted so much time taking calls from angry customers, we have had little time left to tend to the sales objectives." "No," replies the chief technical officer. "We had sign-off from sales leadership six months ago clearly agreeing to keep our launch schedule on plan, in support of the big marketing PR event in Las Vegas. All the press was there. The only way we could hit the date was to cut back on a few features and short-circuit our beta site program. We all knew we were taking risk. What do you want, miracles?"

The CEO, in this theoretical example, is left to pick up the pieces. Where is the accountability? Who botched this up so bad? What am I supposed to say at the board meeting?

Blame and scapegoating, as we know all too well, don't always take the form of department vs. department warfare. In too many cases, people in the organization take the hit. Sales managers, for example, are notorious when ending a bad quarter to select their "poor performers" for layoff. Usually, finding the bad guys is easy pickings. Just look at the league table for who sold the most this past quarter and who sold the least. In fact, look back over the past year to identify the suspect members of the team.

It is seductive for a manager to rationalize that poor individual performance is the key driver of unsatisfactory performance in the aggregate. And by letting a few people go, management demonstrates to everybody watching that poor performance is not tolerated. "We hold people accountable. If you can't cut the mustard, you will be asked to leave."

The All-Too-Familiar Pattern of Blame and Action

Figure 13: Blame and Action

CEOs have, on more than one occasion, attended the board meeting just after a bad quarter to float rhetoric grounded in this illusion of individual accountability. "Yes, we have had a tough quarter. We are not meeting our revenue targets. But rest assured we are holding the sales team accountable. We laid off poor performers and provided a wake-up call to those that remain. Unsatisfactory results will not be tolerated. We are taking action!"

It all sounds a bit childish, doesn't it? But we've seen it in practice again and again. People look to hide, and to deflect blame from themselves onto others. And those who are caught in the trap of blame do everything they can to "act." It doesn't really matter what the actions are, per se, as long as somebody is acting.

Businesses, of course, are driven by revenue and profitability. CFOs and controllers track financial indicators such as growth rates, return on equity, and market share. At the end of the day, it is the firm's performance in the aggregate that counts. No debate is necessary. This is the way business works; everybody understands.

Yet, in the workplace you would never know it. In my judgment, there is a clear gap between espoused theory, i.e. the aspirational chase for financial performance in the aggregate, and theory-in-practice, wherein individual employees act in their own best interests. All too often, individuals are rewarded and punished based on their own contributions or lack thereof.

Salespeople are particularly well placed in an internal contest to deliver personal results. Trophies are given away each year, citing quota club winners and the most outstanding account manager. And salespeople love the accolades, as they post their accomplishments on social media. But non-sales employees also compete for honors and recognition. At the beginning of a new fiscal year, it is routine for management

75

to sit down with employees and review together their individual goals for the coming period. Raises and stock options are at stake, and the staff navigates the corporate landscape to maximize their personal results.

One can argue there is no gap between espoused theory of group performance and the theory-in-practice of individual focus and priority. Those in this camp insist that individual performance, if properly orchestrated, leads to favorable group performance. They are connected by design. It is all intentional. If everybody does their job, then revenue, profit, market share, and other aggregate objectives will follow in a logical, prescribed manner and be fulfilled.

That is the argument underlying almost all traditional KPI-based management strategies. Contemporary management science encourages firms to break down their goals and cascade them all the way down to individual contributors[9]. If everyone does their part, the goal will be met.

Thus, ends here the lesson in management theory. In practice, the outcome is more unpredictable. Why?

Two hypotheses surface as potential explanations. One, underpinning aggregate success is the assumption that high-level goals can be chopped and diced into neat packages for individual consumption. The more complex the team construct, the more difficult the chopping exercise. Since most corporate goals are satisfied through operational execution across functional lines, splitting the atom such that each role

---

[9] https://kpi.org/

in each department is tasked with a purposeful objective, highly correlated to corporate goals, is extraordinarily difficult.

Two, even if goals are successfully chopped and packaged for each individual, danger lies in the literal interpretation of the KPI and associated tasks to maximize individual outcomes. There is an inherent tension between corporate objectives and what an individual wants, such as financial reward, recognition, or simply staying out of trouble.

So, even in the case where senior management gets it right and passes down orderly KPIs to the troops, the people on the ground are still prone to behave, in practical terms, in their best interests. The likely outcomes are obvious and concerning. "Hey, it's not my fault we didn't hit our revenue targets. I did my job." Placing blame, protecting turf, and inventing plausible defensive routines become the new priorities for participants.

Fundamentally, it is tough to reconcile the desire to achieve corporate goals, which by their very nature are team-based, with a management approach that incentivizes, rewards, and celebrates individual behavior.

Business Is a Team Sport

I take a different view. I believe business is a team sport. And from this premise, I reason that the espoused theory of team sport must be aligned, explicitly, with theory-in-practice.

To begin to understand the concept of teamwork in the workplace, let's again consult a definition put forth by Merriam-Webster: "*Work done by several associates with each doing a part but all subordinating personal prominence to the efficiency of the whole."* The notion of subordination is particularly insightful. And, unlike corporate cultures that emphasize hierarchical subordination in the org chart sense, subordination in this context is in respect to a greater good, the whole.

I find it convenient to look to team-based sports for inspiration. Whether at the professional, collegiate, or youth level, coaches in team sports preach teamwork as an axiom for success. It is intuitive to all as observers or participants.

In fact, how curious that famed management consultant Peter F. Drucker said, "The leaders who work most effectively, it seems to me, never say 'I.' And that's not because they have trained themselves not to say 'I.' They don't think 'I.' They think 'we'; they think 'team.' They understand their job to be to make the team function. They accept responsibility and don't sidestep it, but 'we' gets the credit. This is what creates trust, what enables you to get the task done."[10]

Michael Jordan, meanwhile, famously offered, "Talent wins games, but teamwork and intelligence wins championships."[11]

So, if indeed business is a team sport, then why do firms not emphasize teamwork in the same fashion? To me, it is an essential question.

---

[10] https://www.goodreads.com/author/quotes/12008.Peter_F_Drucker

[11] https://www.goodreads.com/author/quotes/16823.Michael_Jordan

What's the Score, Coach?

One clue directing us to a plausible answer may be in the way the scoreboard factors into team play. In basketball, football, lacrosse, hockey, rugby, baseball, soccer, cricket, and every other team sport one can identify, the scoreboard is in full view for players to see together. And the score is always a representation of which team is winning and which is losing at any moment in the contest.

To resolve the question, "Are we winning?" one needs to simply look up at the scoreboard. Yes, we are winning 14-7, or 2-1, or whatever the scoreboard says. There is no ambiguity.

In a business setting, the scoreboard is often hidden from plain sight on a day-to-day basis. When employees ask, "Are we winning?" the answer is typically vague or, at best, framed in a historical context such as last year or last quarter.

It can be very difficult for employees to enjoy the in-the-moment, unambiguous feedback that team sports participants find routine. "What is the score?" can be an awfully elusive question in the workplace.

To fill the vacuum, employees revert to their personal goals, contributions, and results as their pseudo-scoreboard.

Employees in a company look to their OKRs or other personal metrics to connect *their* behavior with *their* scoreboard. If goaled on sales in a specific region or territory, salespeople are very adept at reporting their individual sales to date in relation to their quota. Marketers goaled on a minimum number of leads each month can tell you exactly how they are doing on a week-to-week basis, perhaps even day-to-day.

Folks in administrative functions such as accounting and HR tend to look inward as well, tracking their individual or department level performance as they strive to achieve milestones and hit dates relevant only to them.

The Elusive Scoreboard

Figure 14: The Elusive Scoreboard

The effect carries over to a lack of cooperation, generally, which can be disastrous. The obvious example is the sales department. If you tell salespeople that their pay plan, reputation, and place in the corporate hierarchy are directly tied to their sales performance in their territory, then guess what they focus on? Ask the quota-driven salesperson to help out with a customer in another territory, and you will get resistance, passive or active. Ask them to assist with new-hire assimilation, and you will get, "Not my job, sorry," in reply.

It works the same way with developers and marketers. Tell marketing professionals that their pay plan, reputation, and place in the corporate hierarchy are directly tied to the number of qualified leads they generate, and the goal of reducing the cost per lead 10% over the next six months, then guess what they will focus on? Never mind that sales are down quarter over quarter. If the number of leads is meeting expectations, then, "I am doing my job." The corollary, of course, is, "Someone else must not be doing theirs." Winners and losers compete in a zero-sum game.

But the lack-of-scoreboard phenomenon only partially answers the question of why, in a business setting, teamwork is not emphasized.

The Paradox of Accountability

I believe another idea worthy of consideration is the notion of accountability. Owners expect board members to be accountable for their behavior and results. Board members expect the CEO to be accountable, while CEOs pass on the expectation to senior management. The chain of expectation persists down through the org chart to the very bottom. Everyone, it seems, carries an expectation for accountability.

At first glance, accountability is desirable. The *last* thing we need in *our* company are people who perform at any level they please with impunity. We don't tolerate slackers around here. Everyone pulls their weight!

But looking deeper, the enforcement of accountability carries an unintended (or, perhaps intended?) tendency for blame and scapegoating. When things are going well, subordinates are keen to receive constructive criticism and positive reinforcement from management. Some compete for public credit, while others take on a more passive approach to enjoying their success. But when the shit hits the fan, subordinates experience a very different set of communications from management. Let the games begin. Who did it? Wasn't me. Posturing and vague communication emerge victorious in the battle with truth and clarity.

In a moment of calm, managers in firms that don't meet revenue goals know they must confront a complex set of variables and assumptions. On what basis was the original goal of 35% growth founded? Are the assumptions still valid? If so, why was there no data emerging that signaled the revenue problem sooner? Where did our execution go awry?

Usually, blame and scapegoating contain, collectively, the answer to the question "Why did we not hit our revenue number?" But it is a woefully inefficient way to get at the answer, as senior leadership has to spend a lot of time parsing the blame and filling in the missing pieces. And usually, there are injured personnel along the way. But without teamwork baked into the culture, that's what you get.

So, in summary, I believe companies lack teamwork for two primary reasons. One, it is the absence of a transparent scoreboard to inspire employees' commitment to team goals. Two, it is the perils, unintended as they may be, of individual accountability. The challenge, then, is to mitigate these factors as much as possible.

Compensation Equals Scoreboard

In peer-to-peer culture, we maintain the focus on teamwork through the implementation of a transparent team scoreboard, as well as team-based accountability. Everyone must know the score, understand the rules of the game, and be clear about their role and their impact upon team-based performance.

Nothing says "scoreboard" quite like employee pay plans. As provocative as it may sound, I have found an uncanny causal relationship between team-based pay and team-based results.

Peer-to-Peer Scoreboard

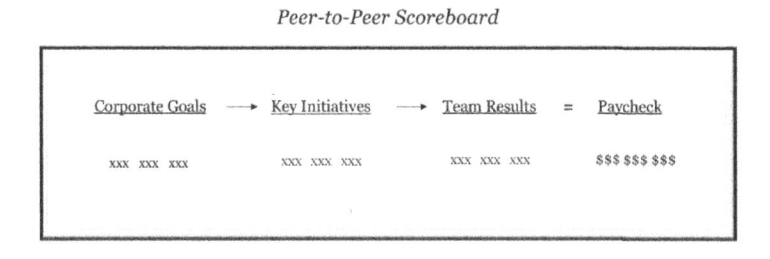

Corporate Goals	→	Key Initiatives	→	Team Results	=	Paycheck
xxx xxx xxx		xxx xxx xxx		xxx xxx xxx		$$$ $$$ $$$

Figure 15: Peer-to-Peer Scoreboard

In our three-year journey when I was CEO, we paid everyone in the company (and I mean everyone) based on a stake in the achievement of corporate objectives. For us, it more resembled a commission structure than a bonus, enabling a tight coupling of behavior, scoreboard, and pay with respect to time. As the score changed day by day with respect to our goals of revenue broken down by category (e.g. product class), we published the results and spoke about them in weekly meetings.

Though everyone was paid according to a confidential individual plan, the criteria used to calculate payout was shared. Our employees were able to see it all happen in a public, transparent manner. Then they could cash in each pay period on the results to date. It was very inspiring for all. I shall discuss more about compensation in a later chapter. The point is, aligning the corporate scoreboard with people's paychecks made the difference in our installation of peer-to-peer culture. The paycheck essentially *became* the corporate scoreboard.

Furthermore, we created a sense of team-based accountability by implementing operational processes that were inherently organized in teams. Teams, cross-functional to the firm, engaged in initiatives conceived to meet corporate goals. Bringing new products to market, for example, required many, many different skill sets, knowledge bases, and parts of the org chart to come together. We did not install, nor maintain, individual goals, but rather emphasized team goals and the associated team-based activity that would prove essential to fulfilling our ambitions.

Teamwork, then, like trust, is something that must be asserted as part of peer-to-peer culture. We talked about it often internally, as well as with customers and potential hires.

Any prejudice or active disagreement by any employee must be confronted and ultimately resolved. Employees must willingly enroll in and comply with cultural expectations. We backed up our assertion for culture with team orientation by installing team-based accountability. We published an active team-based scoreboard with a direct connection to compensation. And we implemented team-based action through cross-functional initiatives.

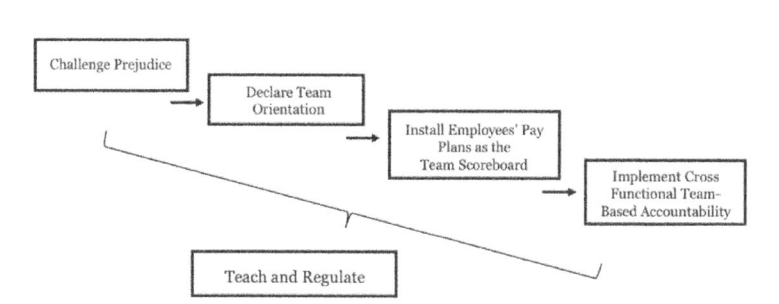

How to Install Teamwork in Peer-to-Peer Culture

- Challenge Prejudice
- Declare Team Orientation
- Install Employees' Pay Plans as the Team Scoreboard
- Implement Cross Functional Team-Based Accountability
- Teach and Regulate

Figure 16: How to Install Teamwork

The rewards were fantastic. To work as a team, and to win as a team, may be the most satisfying thing I have ever done in business.

In Sum

- In a typical corporation, managers look to create space for refuge in the face of trouble. Blame and scapegoating are used as tactics.

- Fundamentally, it is tough to reconcile the desire to achieve corporate goals, which by their very nature are team-based, with a management approach that incentivizes, rewards, and celebrates individual behavior.

- Companies lack teamwork for two primary reasons: One, the absence of a transparent scoreboard to inspire employees' commitment to team goals. Two, the perils, unintended as they may be, of individual accountability. The challenge, then, is to mitigate these factors as much as possible.

- In peer-to-peer culture, maintain the focus on teamwork through the implementation of a transparent team scoreboard, as well as team-based accountability.

- In peer-to-peer culture, the employee's paycheck becomes the critical component of the team scoreboard.

- Create team-based accountability by implementing operational processes organized in cross-functional teams.

Empathy

I have always loathed the notion of negotiation. That is, two parties coming together to outsmart, outdo, and outperform the other party to achieve the best outcome possible as measured by their own interests. The process of buying a car comes to mind, wherein pursuit of the "good deal" is as important as actually purchasing the right vehicle. It's the first question you are asked, when you come home with the keys and are greeted by family and neighbors, "Did you get a good deal?"

The art of negotiation is a subject that has long been analyzed and taught, and rightfully so. In 1968, Chester L. Karrass launched his bestselling training program that still, in the 21st century, commands attention in airline magazines and in C-suites looking to improve the skills of their staff.[12] The message to potential seminar prospects is simple. Attend, and learn the skills required to "win" in a negotiation. Or, considering the other side of the sword, attend so that you don't get out-negotiated in the next encounter. It becomes a matter of pride when entertained in this context. Nobody likes to feel outsmarted, much less swindled, in a business transaction. Indeed, most people approach a negotiation with trepidation. They don't want to end up on the losing end or feel taken. Nobody wants to feel like a fool.

---

[12] https://www.karrass.com/

But there is downside to negotiation with this classic emphasis on winning and losing. Negotiation carries the byproduct of antagonizing relationships. That is, when two parties finish a negotiation, their interpersonal relationship is always different and almost always damaged in some way. Everything is going along swimmingly between vendor and prospect in a sales process until the hard part of the proceedings emerges: when it's time to craft and ultimately agree on the terms of the transaction. Transparency, if it existed, suddenly mutates to opacity. And here again, game theory rears its head. Fans of the movie *Princess Bride* undoubtedly remember the scene in which the characters attempted to outwit each other over the poisoned goblet:[13] "*You only think I guessed wrong! That's what's so funny! I switched glasses when your back was turned!*" The game goes down a rabbit hole of "you are thinking, so therefore I am thinking. But you know what I am thinking, so you are thinking. So therefore, I am thinking in anticipation of what you are thinking."

Two parties, when confronted with a situation wherein they must negotiate an agreement, often behave badly. They hide information. They exaggerate circumstances. They lie. Inevitably a winner emerges while the loser contemplates the outcome, rationalizes the effects, licks their wounds, and resolves to win the next time — perpetuating the cycle. And forever more, the relationship between the parties is changed. The *next* time a negotiation is called for, the parties will go at it with even more bad behavior in hopes that *their* side will come out victorious.

---

[13] https://www.rottentomatoes.com/m/princess_bride

Generally, we tend to envisage negotiation as an act between companies. But there are plenty of negotiations within the walls of a firm taking place every day between people supposedly on the same team. Debates are held and decisions are made often as a direct result of "pitches," power plays, and other selfish acts that warp information. Yes, people also exaggerate, posture, and lie in this environment to win an argument and achieve a desired outcome that may or may not be in the best interest of the firm.

It raises an obvious question. Is this OK? For me, the answer is a swift no. Is it possible to maintain and leverage trusted relationships so that an outcome from negotiation is in the best interest of both parties? And, can we accomplish this feat while maintaining transparency and preserving the relationship? In the end, can we set up a paradigm of negotiation wherein both parties win? As in, really, both win?

Yes, I believe it is possible, as well as desirable. But it requires empathy.

Empathy Is Different From Sympathy

Empathy, as it applies to peer-to-peer culture, is not to be confused with sympathy. It's a critical distinction. Grammar scholars call out sympathy distinctly as *"the ability to take part in someone else's feelings, mostly by feeling sorrowful about their misfortune."*[14] Merriam-Webster describes sympathy as a *"feeling of loyalty: tendency to favor or support."* Sympathy is a fine quality for one to possess, certainly. The world needs sympathetic people. But that's not what I'm talking about

---

[14] https://www.grammarly.com/blog/empathy-sympathy/

here. In business, we don't expect people to go around feeling sorry for colleagues and customers on a regular basis, nor do we want to necessarily favor or support their point of view.

Empathy is more about the ability to understand other people's feelings as if we were having them ourselves. It is your pain, in my heart. It's different than sympathy. To practice empathy, we have to take the other person and what they say seriously. We have to imagine that their situation and their point of view are as legitimate as our situation and point of view. In other words, if we are going to be empathetic, we have to give a shit about the other party and the predicament they find themselves. Ultimately, it's about respect, and unconditional acceptance, that is unaffected by the other's shortcomings or confessions. Do we acknowledge, in sincere terms, that another person has the right to feel the way they do? And can we demonstrate that we understand the other's experience, by describing aspects of it?

If you're thinking, "Gee, this all sounds like psychology," that is because, indeed, empathy is a concept pulled directly from the discipline of psychology. Carl Rogers was one of the most renowned contributors to the field, winning the Award for Distinguished Scientific Contributions by the American Psychological Association in 1956 based on his theories about empathy and what he called "person-centered therapy." He described it as "the effort of a listener to hear the other person deeply, accurately, and nonjudgmentally. One must practice skillful, reflective listening that clarifies and amplifies the person's own experiencing and meaning, without imposing the listener's own material."[15]

Rogers saw the idea with much wider application than therapy. His approach can be used in many settings, including business contexts. Rogers called out three criteria as conditions to practice: congruence, unconditional positive regard, and empathetic understanding.[16] The relevance to interpersonal skills and behaving with empathy in the workplace is uncanny.

Person-Centered Therapy: Core Conditions
Carl Rogers

The therapist is congruent with the client.

The therapist provides the client with unconditional positive regard.

The therapist shows an empathetic understanding to the client.

Figure 17: Carl Rogers' Approach

---

[15] http://cultureofempathy.com/References/Experts/Carl-Rogers-Quotes.htm

[16] Carl Rogers, *Client-Centered Therapy: Its Current Practice, Implications and Theory.* (Constable & Robinson, 1951)

Congruence, essentially, is the manifestation of genuineness. In psychological terms, the therapist, who ordinarily reveals little of their own personality to their client, behaves authentically, to permit the client to experience them as they really are.

Unconditional positive regard, as the words imply, is the ability to accept another person (the client, in Rogers-speak) as they are. One draws a clear distinction between the person, whom we accept unilaterally, and their actions, of which we may or may not approve.

And to practice an empathetic understanding, one must understand accurately, but not sympathetically, the other's experience and feelings in the present. The emphasis is to be in the moment, without regard to history, prejudice, or other influences. The therapist must communicate, clearly, a sense of "I understand."

Once you fully take on the concept of empathy, your perspective on negotiation immediately changes. Why would you strive to run over someone, invalidate their point of view, and attempt to win at their expense in a negotiation? Well, you wouldn't. This sort of behavior flies in the face of acting empathically.

In peer-to-peer culture, wherein we practice empathy, people must be self-aware. They must understand, in the most honest terms possible, the ambiguous situation they are in. What are their constraints, exactly? What is the desired state of clarity in the outcome, and why?

In this model, it's not about winning. It is about optimizing the variables necessary to achieve a mutually desirable outcome.

Then, when two parties who are both self-aware and practicing empathy come to the table to negotiate, they can be free to lay out their constraints and ambitions without fear of retribution. They can say, right out loud, "This is what I need, this is what I want, and this is where I am constrained."

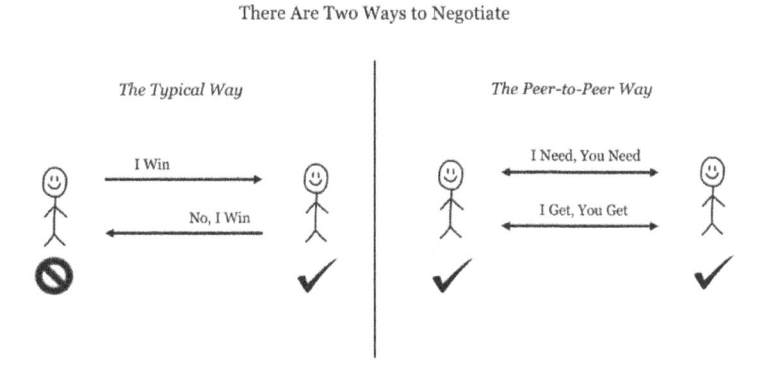

There Are Two Ways to Negotiate

The Typical Way | The Peer-to-Peer Way
I Win / No, I Win | I Need, You Need / I Get, You Get

Figure 18: Alternatives in Negotiation

If both parties describe their point of view in a trusted manner, sincere brainstorming can take place to achieve the best outcome for *both* parties. And in so doing, the integrity of the relationship is also optimized forward. Essentially, both parties accept an outcome that is less than perfect, and probably less than their best-case desired outcome. But they value the relationship more. Empathy wins, rather than one party at the expense of the other.

How It Works In Practice: An Example

A powerful example comes from my personal experience. With the sales executive in tow, we made an important visit to a major customer who had found themselves in a bit of a predicament. The customer had purchased our products a few years back and had enjoyed great success. In fact, perhaps they enjoyed too much success, as they were using more of our products than they had paid for. A new contract would be required, or else the customer risked a breach. The customer was embarrassed and wanted to resolve the situation while minimizing exposure. It was an innocent mistake; there was no need to cause undo harm or get people in trouble. However, the customer had no mid-year budget set aside for this kind of purchase. It would have to come from a discretionary fund and require an internal proposal and approval process.

The sales exec and I approached the meeting with empathy for their situation. But we were firm in our position that they owed us more money, or else we would have to downgrade their use. We were direct. As were they.

> **Us:** We are so happy that you are using our products to such a large extent, but we must resolve the contract issue in short order.

> **Customer:** We know. This is so embarrassing. The problem is this is all unexpected and unplanned.

Us: What funds do you have access to?

Customer: We have looked at this hard and believe we can steal $500,000 from another budget that has some excess money. But that's it. Anything more would have to be postponed until next year and require a fresh look from senior management about why we are using your products and not similar products used by our sister division.

Us: It is in both our interests to resolve the matter swiftly and keep all drama at bay. In fact, we don't want to go through this again. Suppose we give you a contract upgrade that provides unconstrained use of our products for $500,000. As you know, this sort of upgrade is worth more like $1 million based on what you have spent so far. But we think it would be the best way out of the jam. All we'd ask is that you and your team would take an active role in our marketing activity to speak on our behalf at industry events and take reference calls for our other prospects. We will also need the $500,000 transaction to be closed this month. How does that sound?

Customer: That is very kind of you to offer such a great deal on the $500,000. And yes, we can get it done quickly and support you forward. We love working with your team. We just need to work the internal process; it might take some time until we can get a purchase order.

Us: Awesome. We have a deal. What is the holdup on the process, do you think?

Customer: We have a bunch of forms to fill out online and justification to document. I am so jammed the next few days; I won't have time to attend to it until next Monday.

Us: Well, we've been very efficient in this meeting so far. We had an hour budgeted and have only used 10 minutes. Why not give it a go right now? We can help you craft the prose while we are all here together.

And at this point in the negotiation, the customer opened a laptop and we proceeded to fill out the forms together, including the exercise to write the justification for the upgrade. We completed it within the hour, the customer processed it swiftly, and we had a purchase order the next week.

Give-Get

Empathy, as it turns out, is practiced in peer-to-peer culture with an additional, corresponding responsibility. People must be their own advocates. Empathy is not just about relating to and respecting others' point of views. As a direct consequence of self-awareness, people must also continuously look for opportunities to communicate *their* needs, wants, and constraints, honestly, in the day-to-day operations of the business. I call it "give-get."

It is simple enough. Ask for something before you respond to a request to give something. In its reciprocal form, you should expect the other party to also ask for something before giving to you.

This is not meant to be sleazy. Quid pro quo is the Latin phrase that means an exchange of goods or services, in which one transfer is contingent upon the other; "a favor for a favor." Quid pro quo can lead to pay for performance, or pay for access, and when taken to its natural extension, is a bribe. Unequivocally, that is not what I am suggesting with give-get.

I prefer phrases such as "give and take" to describe the phenomenon. It is a fair exchange, given freely with no moral compromise, framed in empathy.

In business culture, establishing a communication protocol based upon a give-get paradigm can anchor a trusted and honest relationship. We are not talking about favors for favors, in the unscrupulous sense. Give-get means that I communicate with you in a way that we exchange mutual understanding, and our requests with each other remain in balance.

As Applied to the Sales Department

The behavior of salespeople provides a good example. They typically love to respond to requests from a customer. Customers ask, salespeople respond. "Can we schedule a product demo sometime in the next few weeks?" asks the department manager employed by the prospective customer. "By all means," responds the salesperson, at the ready. "Let's get our calendars out and get this scheduled. Sounds great."

"I don't see the problem," you may be thinking. After all, if a prospect is keen to see a product demo, then we should certainly oblige. It's a good thing, right? Maybe. But, thinking a step ahead, our objective should be to ensure a positive outcome of the product demo, rather than simply executing the duty as a stage performer. And if we are honest in reflection, indeed there are some things we can identify now that will affect the way the demo experience progresses. For instance, who will be in the room?

Take the scenario in which we expect the core project team to be in attendance, probably six people in total. The manager is generally favorable in her outlook about the idea of doing business together within the next few months. She likes what she has seen so far and has asked for the demo to be set up. Four of the people in the meeting will be new to the party. None of them have, as far as we know, taken much of a glance at our product yet. But the final member of the team we expect in attendance is someone we've met. This guy has been a bit of a stick in the mud, in fact. We have met him twice so far in the sales cycle and each time, he seems content to defend the status quo and call our product into question. "Why do we even need your product?" he asks. "We are fine

98

now using what we've got. And besides, the skill set of all the team members is firmly rooted in the current product installation. We don't have the time to learn something new."

A decision must be made, at the exact moment the manager asks the salesperson to set up the demonstration meeting. He can rush to "yes," and scramble to open the calendar app in his phone. Or he can consider the give-get paradigm, practicing empathy, and ask for something before committing to the meeting. "Yes, if I were in your position, I would feel the same way. Sharing a wider understanding across your team about our product is an excellent next step. But I have had a couple of encounters with your project manager, Mario. It seems Mario is a bit shy with respect to the idea of change and is wedded to the status quo for whatever reason. I would love to book the demo, but can I ask you to please keep Mario well behaved during the meeting? He will, I fear, attempt to pollute the spirit of the meeting by vocalizing his concerns in an unfair manner. It will ultimately be your decision to buy our product or not. And Mario's opinion will be something you have to consider. I understand."

Give-get, delivered with empathy. It is a balanced, open, and honest dialogue, not the sort that customers generally experience. Tone is important, certainly in the way a salesperson expresses their give-get question. Damage would surely be done if the salesperson implied threat or showed arrogance with a phrase such as, "I am only doing a demo if Mario is not invited." I am not suggesting the give-get paradigm is one where the salesperson feels free to exhibit undue authority or control. But if communicated with an empathetic voice, the salesperson is rewarded for consistently asking for consideration and action before complying with customer requests.

Micro-Agreements

The give-get paradigm offers the chance to create an ongoing dialogue whereby the parties continuously are forced to agree or abort the process. Let's call these ongoing agreements "micro-agreements."

Rather than putting forth all the effort to realize the all-or-nothing big agreement, (e.g. buy or don't buy), the pursuit of micro-agreements emphasizes a more authentic line of communication. In this manner, when parties *do* get to the end of the negotiation, it is merely a step, rather than some intimidating, bigger than life event.

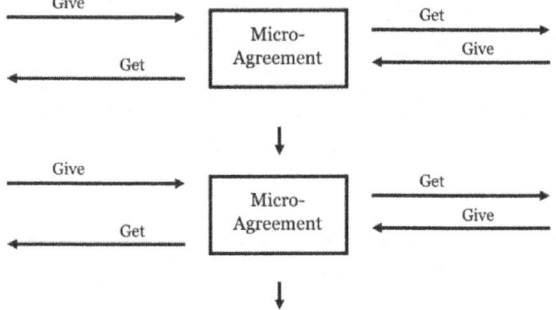

Figure 19: Micro-Agreements

Micro-agreements build on each other, as give and get conversations roll on. Everyone's needs, wants, and constraints are communicated, and resolved to the best degree possible, as a matter of course through time, in a natural and trusted fashion.

The give-get mindset can become addictive. Each party should feel free to reflectively pursue a counter request to every request received. In the case of internal dialogue, debates, and negotiations, the process becomes routine. The interesting part for me to observe has been the effect on customer relationships, particularly prospects. Usually, they don't expect it. It can be a bit arresting. But when a salesperson has shown the way, and asked for micro-agreements from the outset, the prospect learns to ask their fair share. A salesperson asks, "Can I request we get a meeting with your vice president? I would love to get her in the loop for preapproval." Rather than offering a yes/no to this question, a prospect can say, "I agree that would be a good step. But I am only comfortable seeking pre-approval if your development team agrees to pull in the 'Ajax feature' we need. You have said December is the likely date for release. But we need it in August. Can you ask your CTO about it in advance of the meeting?" Both parties act in balance, mutually seeking to resolve the key obstacles visible at present.

Note that from the vendor's point of view, in this example, they may *not* be able to pull in the desired feature to August. If not, then the prospect is free to cancel the step to meet the VP. In fact, the entire sales cycle may be aborted. But more likely, some form of compromise will emerge. The important point is the integrity of the relationship between salesperson and prospect is preserved. There is no guessing. There are no games.

Installing Empathy

Installing empathy in peer-to-peer culture takes a similar path as other attributes.

We first must confront employee prejudice, usually found in the new hire. We declare empathy as a behavioral expectation. We teach the Rogers approach and install hard practices with respect to give-get and continuously seeking to form behavioral contracts, called micro-agreements internally, as well as externally in customer engagements.

How to Install Empathy in Peer-to-Peer Culture

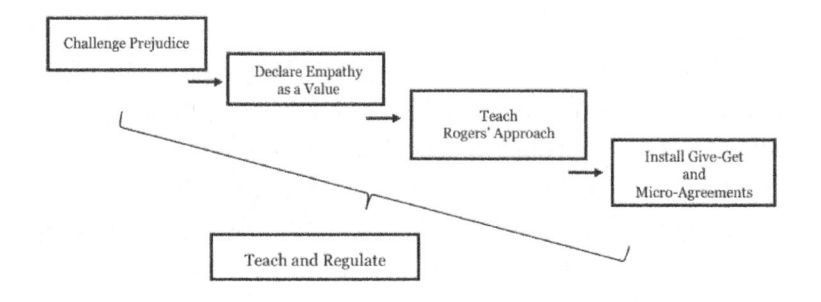

Figure 20: How to Install Empathy

Practicing empathy in peer-to-peer culture also creates a healthy resistance to stress. The culture creates a bit of a safety net. Stress can advance a weakened state of mind, sometimes debilitating, for staff and customers alike. Without question, people under stress behave in unpredictable ways, as the mind is clouded with what-ifs, worry, and consternation. And once people go into an altered state, coping mechanisms emerge that are not always productive. We can all recall, from our own experience, shouting matches, pouting, and door-slamming episodes. Passive aggressive behavior can also, too often, find its way forward. And it's not just between team members of an organization. Customer relationships exhibit the same characteristics when the situation screams of problems. Late shipments, systems down, and other factors prompt customers to turn up the heat on a vendor.

In a peer-to-peer culture enjoying the fruits of empathy, those that share concerns are more routinely greeted with understanding. But more importantly, the group shares in the stress, mitigating its effect on each person individually. "We are all in this together" is a powerful mantra. And when colleagues practice empathy with colleagues, and vendors practice empathy with customers, the opportunity to work together toward resolution when trouble appears is vivid. Implied intent is absent. Judgments of wrongdoing are kept at bay. Dialogue is positive in tone, even if the content of the discussion is negative. And more times than not, a solution worthy of pursuing is nominated, implemented, and celebrated.

Empathy. It's a beautiful thing.

In Sum

- There is downside to negotiation done with the classic emphasis on winning and losing. Negotiation carries a byproduct of antagonizing relationships.

- Negotiation can be done in the interest of both parties when empathy is used. The quality of empathy I am stressing is more about the ability to understand other people's feelings as if we were having them ourselves. It is your pain, in my heart.

- Psychologist Carl Rogers identified three conditions to practice what he called "person-centered therapy": congruence, unconditional positive regard, and empathetic understanding.

- Empathy is practiced in peer-to-peer culture with an additional, corresponding responsibility. People must be their own advocates.

- Give-get means that we communicate in a way that we exchange mutual understanding, and our requests of each other remain in balance.

- The give-get paradigm creates an ongoing dialogue whereby the parties continuously are forced to agree or abort the process. Let's call these ongoing agreements "micro-agreements.

Honesty

Conflict, along with its companion, confrontation, are natural phenomena found in nature. Think *National Geographic* or television shows about the natural world for a second, and images of kill-or-be-killed animal behavior springs to mind. The business world is not exempt. The hard truth is that conflict is as much a part of running a business as invoices and budgets. Inevitably, something goes wrong. And usually, people are involved.

In a business setting, a state of conflict can take many forms. Expressions of anger, particularly when delivered to excess, are an easy kind to spot. More subtle varietals are camouflaged in rudeness, abruptness, and pointed sarcasm. And when group communication begins to drown in moaning, grumbling, and whining, a conflict is usually simmering. Email and other electronic media tend to enhance the effect, as people use them to "say" things they wouldn't dream of saying out loud, face to face. Sometimes such expressions are petty, and not symptomatic of a conflict. But often, they are.

Resolving conflict, independent of the source, is always a chore. It is a leap into confrontation, to one degree or another. Someone must take the first, awkward step. That is, somebody must call out the conflict and initiate an attempt to resolve it. Blind escalation, in which one goes to a boss or other authority for resolution without taking the matter up with the participants, is sometimes required. Someone harassed in the workplace, for example, has every right to singularly escalate to HR or legal authorities. But usually, blind escalation is correlated with inflammatory outcomes. The informant is a tattletale. Relationships can be damaged, potentially irrevocably.

Most people understand, in the abstract, that confronting the people who are directly associated with the issue at hand offers the best chance for resolution, while minimizing corporate drama. If escalation is required, we go to the boss together, not behind someone's back. The process should be straightforward. Identify the issue, call it out for what it is, confront the person or people in the best position to fix or improve the issue, escalate in harmony if required, implement the change, and voila, problem solved. It if it were only so easy.

We all know that confronting someone can be a very difficult proposition. Consider the circumstance faced by many families: "Aunt Suzy sure drinks a lot. She is late to work more and more. I think she has a problem." Yet, in this example, the family avoids confrontation. Enrollment into a rehabilitation program might be in order, but nobody in the family is willing to confront Aunt Suzy. And I don't think it can be dismissed simply as lazy behavior. Sure, it might be representative of a family that operates in a let-it-be paradigm. But the more likely condition is one of conflict aversion. Nobody wants to initiate the dialogue because of fear. The idea of conflict can be scary for people. So, what happens to Aunt Suzy? Nothing. We kick the can down the road in the false hope that the problem will somehow magically resolve itself.

Not surprisingly then, when we all go to work, our fears and prejudices about conflict and confrontation that we learn at home accompany us. We cannot escape them. People fortunate enough to come from environments in which conflict is an accepted condition, and confrontation is a normal, productive routine, are in a strong position. Many are not so fortunate, having been the victims of abusive relationships, or simply raised in households in which "we don't talk about difficult matters." People are who they are, in all shapes and sizes, holding dramatically different perceptions about how to deal with conflict.

Confrontation at the Office Can Be Hard

So, what are we supposed to do to achieve a course correction when issues at the office need attention? Passive approaches are not terribly forthright and too often fail to resolve much of anything. Familiar scenarios (i.e. games) take place wherein information is withheld, cliques materialize, and meetings are held that conveniently ignore to invite undesirable attendees.

All the better to confront, then, right? Shouldn't a commitment to confronting difficult situations be our standard for corporate behavior? Well, as they say, it's complicated.

In a typical corporate environment, where individual accountability is stressed, confrontation routinely invokes defensive routines in the recipient. It's all too personal. People feel like they must defend themselves. They get mad. They bring up old, harbored feelings and stories long buried, but nonetheless lingering and now somehow relevant, to explain away the issues they face. They deflect blame and accuse others of ill will and bad behavior. They make excuses.

We are taught to separate the person from the issue. Carl Rogers, along with his theories, is again entirely relevant.

"Unconditional positive regard" implies we can love the person but hate their actions.

But in reality, separating the person from the issue can be very difficult. Feelings of being picked on and attacked dominate the psyche of the confronted person. Maybe the confronted person is skilled enough to deflect the perceived assault in a productive manner. Usually, negative emotions prevail, and dialogue becomes bumpy, even raw. Relationships are damaged, temporarily in the best case and permanently in the worst.

But matters in the workplace requiring confrontation persist week in and week out. We have to deal with them one way or another. Employee performance problems offer a good example, as they often create a nasty challenge for everyone involved. Colleagues close to the situation (and sometimes even customers) will often see the issue first, holding expressed opinions such as, "Prudence isn't pulling her weight. When is Maverick going to get some nerve and deal with it? She should have been fired months ago." Everybody that works in Prudence's office sees it. Maverick may even see it.

But Mav is not looking forward to confronting Pru, much less firing her. He is all too aware of the prescribed process he'll have to follow and, in doing so, confess his lack of documentation covering Prudence's history demanded by Nick in HR. Is she clear about her role? Does she know precisely what she's supposed to do, or could she argue her to-do list is vague? Is she getting what she needs to perform at a satisfactory level from management and colleagues? "Oh, no. This is going to be a messy undertaking," muses Mav. "I'm really not sure I have the appetite or the time to take this on."

So, Prudence stays with the firm, continuing to perform in a poor manner. Morale in the department takes a hit. All while the boss goes into denial, or hopes the issue will be resolved somehow, without confrontation, as if to will an improved state by pixie dust.

In peer-to-peer culture, we recognize that stuff goes wrong all the time. It's nobody's fault. Shit happens. As CEO, I always expect the group to be struggling with intractable problems. But there are invariably a set of people close to the issue, either as participants in a compromised process or recipients of undesirable or incorrect output from a broken process, that see the problem for what it is. Is the problem worth fixing? Sometimes not, if a matter is deemed immaterial, a one-time fluke, or simply explained away as unlucky. But if the problem *is* worth fixing, the spell must be broken. Somebody must initiate the act of confrontation.

To confront is the right choice. We want a culture in which people "see it, say it, and confront it." But we want to confront successfully, ensuring maximum attention is paid to the issues at hand for speedy remedy. We want to minimize personal attacks, judgments, and other forms of agitation that provoke unproductive, defensive routines. And, we want to stay miles away from breaches of HR policies or legal boundaries.

It seems daunting. How, exactly, do we overcome our natural aversion and pull off such a tricky proposition as practicing confrontation successfully?

By subscribing to the attribute of honesty.

What It Means To Be Honest

The idea of practicing confrontation in the workplace with honest tone is not a new one. Our friend Andy Grove, former CEO of technology giant Intel, called the matter "constructive confrontation." In his book *High Output Management*[17], Grove maintained that all communication, however nice or unpleasant the subject, must proceed objectively. Opinions must be defended with data, and debate should ensue without regard to title or position in a corporate hierarchy. Nobody gets a pass; all decisions can be challenged.

But once the debate is over, Grove advocated a "disagree and commit" notion that essentially called the winners from the losers, brought order from chaos, and pushed the team forward, at least under the illusion of agreement. It wasn't a bad model, clearly, based on the exquisite performance that the company has shown for decades.

Much like with the attribute of trust, in which we make an assertion that the value will be upheld and practiced in peer-to-peer culture, honesty takes on the same form, with the same high priority. We simply declare that, as things go wrong (and they will), we expect an honest voice to initiate a confrontation for understanding, analysis, and remedy.

Calling again on our sources for semantics and grammar, we find the definition of honesty to be one *free from fraud or deception. Legitimate. Truthful.*[18]

---

[17] Andrew S. Grove, *High Output Management* (Vintage Books, 1983)

[18] https://www.merriam-webster.com/dictionary/honest

Indeed, in peer-to-peer culture, the quest for truth is the key to the whole affair. We accept employees in the spirit of trust and teamwork to be well-meaning. Their intent, in other words, is always taken as sincere, and to be in the best interest of the company. We reject, as a matter of principle, the notion that people behave in a manner contrary to the firm's best interests.

Therefore, in the workplace, we declare the truth in the idea that something that has gone wrong, despite the best intentions of the team. What went wrong, by definition, is not subject to blame, judgment, or reproach. It was a breakdown in process, understanding, access to information, or a host of other reasons. But it's nobody's fault.

And if it's nobody's fault, we can get on with the discussion about what happened, why it happened, and what we can do to fix it without antagonizing people's feelings or invoking unproductive defensive routines. We can confront the issues. We can speak with honesty.

Fault and blame are clearly not helpful concepts, with their pejorative tone and implication of witch hunts. In peer-to-peer culture, we reject them.

But culpability, I find, is a useful term as we apply it to peer-to-peer. American law is, in part, based on the Model Penal Code, in which four levels of culpability are defined: purposely, knowingly, recklessly, and negligently.[19] For our purposes, I add a fifth level grounded in naivete. Sometimes there is

---

[19] https://www.ali.org/media/filer_public/23/5d/235db86d-f32c-4b7a-b441-b714a53c7981/mpc-culpability-requirements-202.pdf

absolutely no intention, nor awareness of one's behavior effecting a negative outcome. It is simply an accident.

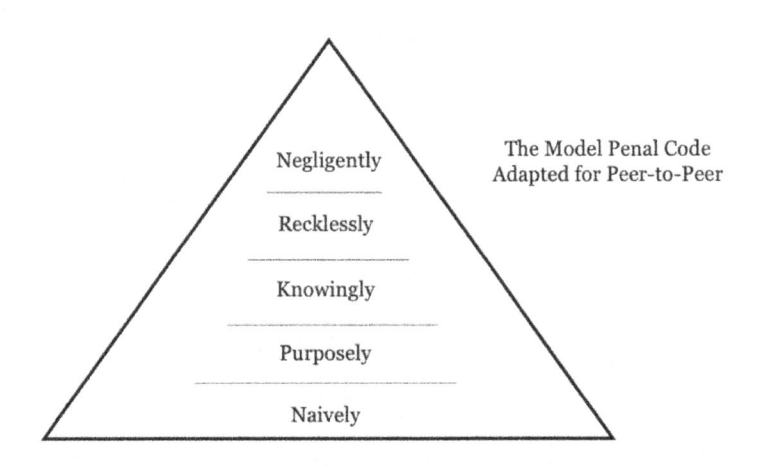

```
                    /\
                   /  \
                  / Negligently \        The Model Penal Code
                 /--------\              Adapted for Peer-to-Peer
                / Recklessly \
               /--------------\
              /   Knowingly    \
             /------------------\
            /     Purposely      \
           /----------------------\
          /        Naively         \
         /--------------------------\
```

Figure 21: Model Penal Code

Employees should ask, "What did I do, or not do, to contribute to the situation in which we find ourselves?" It is part of the diagnosis process, as well as promoting learning, behavioral reprograming, and healing. Owning up to one's culpability is part of being honest, and something we expect from adults in peer-to-peer culture.

I should clarify that peer-to-peer culture, as I describe it, differs somewhat from the ideas and methods installed by Grove at Intel.

While he insisted on confrontational dialogue maintaining a commitment to constructiveness, the cultural attribute he prescribed does not overtly make the distinction between people and issues. As long as one is constructive and holds their opinions in check with facts and data, attacking someone and assigning blame are legitimate tactics in the fight, as I recall from my days as an employee under his command.

For all of Intel's success, management gained a reputation of ruthlessness and communicating with brutal bluntness, deserved or not. But for me, confrontation is not merely a matter of communicating with bluntness. It is more about discovery, analysis, and resolution of issues among trusted teammates.

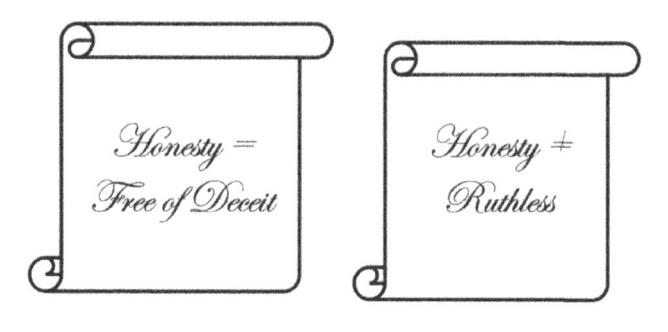

Figure 22: Honesty Is Not Ruthless

In peer-to-peer culture, we are able to leverage the foundational attributes of trust and teamwork, as well as empathy. Practicing the art of confrontation with honesty works very much in concert with these ideals.

For us during our journey, declaring honesty as a cultural value was an important first step. But I found in practical terms, successful implementation required good technique in the way we communicated. We had to teach it, model it, reward it, and help people get better at it every day. To find it, I go back to a guy who had something to say on this subject nearly a century ago.

Putting It Into Practice

Dale Carnegie, back in 1936, became a business cult celebrity based on his book *How to Win Friends and Influence People*.[20] The "Carnegie sandwich" was posited as a three-layer approach to a confrontational moment in the life of a businessperson. First, say something nice to get the recipient warmed up. Then, deliver the essence of the feedback in direct language. Finally, wrap it up with another positive remark to soften the blow. Bingo, bango, bongo.

All is supposedly achieved without hurting anyone's feelings. It's no wonder modern management teams have created the slang term "shit sandwich" to describe the phenomenon. The approach just reeks of manipulation and gamesmanship.

---

[20] Dale Carnegie, *How to Win Friends and Influence People* (Simon & Schuster, 1936)

A Stale Sandwich, Indeed

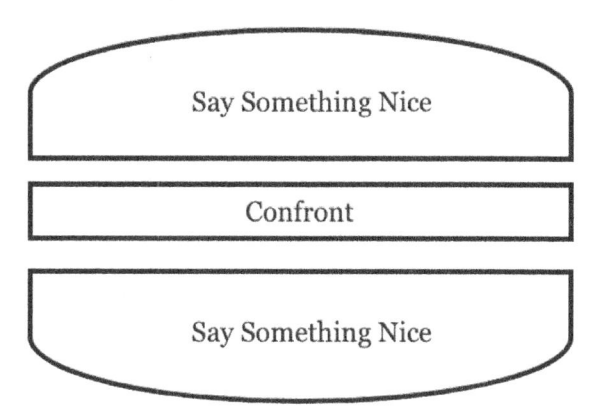

Figure 23: A Stale Sandwich

But Carnegie was on to something when he suggested that a three-step technique was required to maximize effectiveness of an act of confrontation. Bookending a hard message with compliments and distraction is kind, except for the manipulative part. But Carnegie's three-layer approach is worthy in the abstract. We adopt his structure in the implementation of honest confrontation in a peer-to-peer organization.

The first step is an expression of empathy. To assume the receiving party has the same view as the delivering party is absurd. So, let's recognize the difference in the opening. "I don't see the world through the same lens as you, Emily. I realize your point of view about how we generate leads at a trade show is more quantitative than qualitative. I get it, and certainly like the idea of lots of leads. Even if they don't buy in the short term, these contacts are useful to target for ongoing communications. Who knows, maybe they turn into customers down the road."

The opening is completed. Emily's viewpoint is validated, not dismissed, as the confrontation is initiated.

The second step is to segue to the matter at hand: the conflict itself. But before just blasting into it, the confronting party must be swift to point to a specific team goal.

Engaging in Peer-to-Peer Honesty

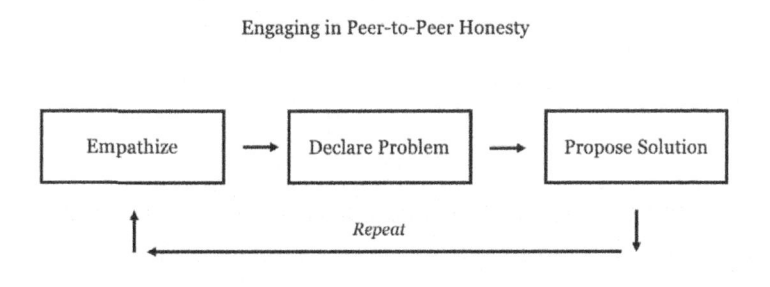

Empathize → Declare Problem → Propose Solution

↑ ←—————— Repeat ——————→ ↓

Figure 24: Peer-to-Peer Honesty

"But Emily, I'm worried about achieving our revenue goals we've set up for the new product line, Spider." It's a statement Emily can't dispute. She understands that the Spider launch is important for the firm, and a revenue ramp is essential. All that is stated so far is, "I'm concerned." From here, the door is open to describe the core of the conflict. If the power of peer-to-peer culture is working, Emily is listening with objectivity. "In my opinion, we are missing a golden opportunity to engage prospects about Spider in the trade show booth. Sure, we have the signs up and they look good. But the demo is weak, and the staff is underprepared to deal with the complexity of the conversations. Prospects get counted as leads, sure. But they don't have that aha moment that spikes their interest in Spider."

At this stage, is Emily prone to be defensive? Doubtful. More likely, she is keen to hear more. The final, third step of the technique unfolds to propose a resolution in the team-oriented paradigm. "In my opinion, we need to overhaul the demo. And we must make sure we have two to three technical people at all the shows to properly engage the prospects. Yes, it will be more expensive to fund these talented resources to stand in a booth all day. And the number of leads per show won't go up, necessarily. But we will drive new business for Spider. I am convinced."

What, exactly, would be the outcome of this debate with Emily? Who knows? The point is, a conflict has been initiated by confrontation anchored in honesty. The dialogue is free from personal attack and devoid of defensive routines. The best possible resolution is debated and installed. Trust persists and teamwork is maintained.

Let's go back to the tough problem of managing our poor performers. We can construct a productive scenario for constructive confrontation in the same way as we did with Emily and our hypothetical lead generation example. When confronting an employee with the action of termination, the three-step process works the same way. Empathize, describe the core problem, then offer the resolution.

"Philip, I understand from your point of view you joined us here at Pico Systems with great enthusiasm. You were attracted to our team culture and have committed yourself to be a good teammate throughout. But you are not keeping up with the volume of work that is required or that is delivered by your teammates. The team is suffering because of it. We've tried for weeks now to improve the situation with training and assigning a one-on-one content expert. It makes me sad we haven't been able to do it. Unfortunately, I'm going to have to let you go. I will assist in any way I can in your pursuit of your next opportunity. For now, I'll send you to Hank in HR to talk through your severance package."

Confrontation with an honest voice has been an important component of peer-to-peer culture as I lived it. The sooner we identified issues holding back our ambitions, the sooner we confronted them, and the sooner we got on with an improved situation. We got better, every day.

By empowering employees in your firm to "see it, say it, and confront it," as a routine part of their daily behavior, you can truly unleash the pursuit of excellence. Who knows? Maybe you and your team will enjoy it as much as we did.

In Sum

- Resolving conflict, independent of the source, is always a chore. It is a leap into confrontation, to one degree or another. Someone must take the first, awkward step.

- In a typical corporate environment wherein individual accountability is stressed, confrontation routinely invokes defensive routines in the recipient. It's all too personal.

- In peer-to-peer culture, the quest for truth is the key to the whole affair. We accept employees in the spirit of trust and teamwork to be well-meaning.

- To confront in peer-to-peer, we empathize, declare the problem honestly, and propose a solution in good faith.

- Employees should "see it, say it, and confront it" as a routine part of their daily behavior.

Dynamic Action

Call it a pet peeve if you must. But I can't stand the way many companies operate, burdened with a lot of BS. I've encountered my fair share over my career. You know what I mean, where stern process seems to dominate the landscape. And where employees, so focused on adhering to these processes, push the buttons on their phones and keyboards at a steady pace. They check email. They go to meetings, one after another, as if their attendance somehow justifies their place in the organization and their worth to the firm. They engage in social media and other distractions. Whatever employees do, in this sort of organization, they don't rock the boat. They don't commit to anything beyond the immediate scope of their roles unless they absolutely have to. They do their jobs, try to be diplomatic, and avoid screwing anything up.

I make two observations about these sorts of corporate environments. One: Employees, more often than not, communicate with each other using language that is vague. Furthermore, they posture. Two: Decision-making policy, with its eye on preservation of management authority, often precludes those on the ground, close to the action, from making a call to resolve an exceptional circumstance outside their restricted power.

Let's first consider the communication issue.

Eh, What Did You Say?

We can all see the value in the phrase "say what you mean and mean what you say." It's common sense. But I find people don't speak plainly and clearly in the workplace. They fill the air with excessive language and use code words and acronyms. Simple questions such as, "Will the product be ready to ship on Friday?" are met with ambiguous answers, like, "We're doing everything we can to make it happen." Sales management can get a song and dance when inquiring of the sales associate, "Is Acme going to close by the end of the month?" The answer might be posed as, "It should close, they really love the product." Huh? Not sure I understand that answer.

Why are people vague and evasive? Why the focus on imprecise language such as buzzwords, labels, and acronyms?

For one, it is because folks often don't understand the details and nuances of the business well enough to offer a clear, confident point of view. Newcomers to a corporate environment are routinely blown away with the amount of secret language bandied about. "There is so much to learn," one mutters when starting a fresh role with a new firm. But before too many months go by, the intimidation wanes, and one is left to realize that much of what is spoken are just vague references to concepts that people don't comprehend as well as they might think. Words such as "enablement" and phrases such as "go-to-market" attempt to put simple labels on concepts that, in fact, are very complex.

The more people use the labels, the less they must talk about the complexity. "We are scheduling a meeting this afternoon to discuss the go-to-market objectives for our new rocket-ship product." What the hell does that mean? Will we be discussing revenue objectives, PR plans, beta site testing criteria, sales training, or what?

But I think there's more to it than explaining away vague communication simply by accepting people's lack of understanding because of challenges presented by new assignments or new jobs. As people settle into their roles, they form perceptions about how they relate to teammates and comprehend what's going on around them. Yet, they can still be ambiguous when they communicate, affecting others in their path as misunderstanding spreads to a wider group. It is particularly painful when the misunderstanding finds its way to a customer.

No, I think there is a much deeper phenomenon at work. People use important-sounding words, high-order abstractions, and passive construction because there is a perceived social cost to being clear. It becomes a form of dishonesty, to one degree or another. Communication is insincere at a minimum, and perhaps devious.

I wonder: What is the perceived social cost that prevents people from being clear and direct?

The answer, I think, stems from the paradigm created in firms in which employees are assigned roles on an org chart. Behavior takes on a form of acting. Fred, in the workplace, tries to act as the senior director of partner marketing, rather than behaving as, well, Fred. Whatever he *really* thinks about the circumstances, challenges, and other people in the firm takes a back seat to the act.

But it's not an act whereby Fred simply reads his lines, as if cast in a theatrical play. No, he gets to improvise pretty much any way he wants, as long as he interacts with others within the constraints of corporate policy and the expectation for how his role as senior director contributes to operational processes. Oh, and he must perform his role as flawlessly as possible. Or else.

The "or else" clause, though unspoken day to day, is always there. Individual accountability, prevalent in companies today, is a direct assault on our place within Maslow's hierarchy.

Abraham Maslow is regarded as one of the most influential psychologists of the 20th century.[21] A New Yorker born in 1908, Maslow observed that "the fundamental desires of human beings are similar despite the multitude of conscious desires."[22]

In fact, Maslow contends, all humans have needs that can be stacked in priority. It is only when one has fulfilled the requirements to survive (think: air, water, food, and shelter), that they are free to focus on a concern for safety. And only when safe does one crave love. Esteem and, finally, the ability to "self-actualize," complete the model in an ascending order of perpetual dependency on the fulfillment of lower levels.

---

[21] https://positivepsychology.com/abraham-maslow/

[22] https://www.liebertpub.com/doi/10.1089/jpm.2006.9.1120; Zalenski & Raspa, 2006

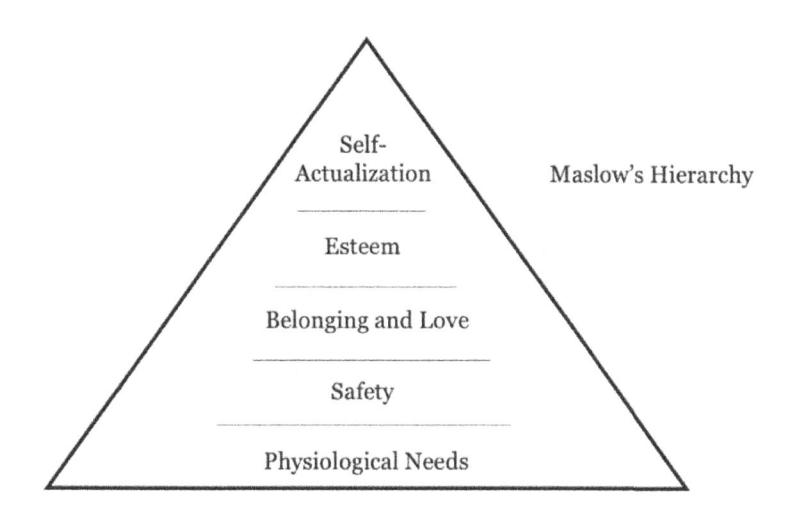

```
                    /\
                   /  \
                  / Self- \
                 /Actualization\         Maslow's Hierarchy
                /----------------\
               /     Esteem       \
              /--------------------\
             /   Belonging and Love  \
            /------------------------\
           /         Safety            \
          /----------------------------\
         /      Physiological Needs      \
        /--------------------------------\
```

Figure 25: Maslow's Hierarchy

It is the need to survive, and the need to be secure, that must be resolved before any higher-level needs are in the mix. If survival and security are compromised, all the rest of it is out the window.

When we feel secure, we want to thrive. The workplace offers us the chance to do both, as it offers security to our lives from compensation and intrinsic satisfaction from our contributions.

When security is threatened, we behave with self-interest. We stay clear of trouble by avoiding accountability anywhere we can, knowing that failure leads to blame, and blame leads to consequences. So, we are vague, use excessive words, and attempt to deflect responsibility in our communication.

Further, in an effort to create separation between us, the winners and them, the losers, we become self-promoters. We posture.

Posturing

Often characterized as "tooting one's own horn," bragging and boasting are too familiar to most corporate conversations in which the declaration of winners and losers looms large. However, posturing is a real killer of successful communication. In a corporate culture that rewards individual achievement and scapegoating when things go bad, people look for public opportunities to engage in self-promotion. "Look at what I did" is offered by an employee in the hope that others will validate the accomplishment publicly. And once validated by the group, the accomplishment becomes part of the employee's brand as they look for advancement on the org chart, increased power, or to be held in higher esteem by a boss or other person in the org chart.

Psychologists would certainly argue that most people, acting out of positive intent, need explicit positive feedback to fulfill the simple human need for approval and validation. Everyone loves an attaboy. Those who, for whatever reason, don't receive enough praise from third parties fill the void by supplying it themselves. They brag and boast for self-fulfillment. In moderation, or when emphasizing contributions largely attributed to the group, demonstrating some swagger is harmless and usually considered playful by colleagues.

Bragging, however, when done to excess, is the work of the narcissist. And narcissists, with their need so deeply wired into their psyches that no amount of validation is ever enough, adopt posturing as routine. In peer-to-peer culture, this behavior presents a real problem. It is outlier behavior that must be corrected through rehabilitation or removed from the culture through termination.

The Effects of Power

Relative power possesses an important, obvious effect on communication. Speaking in a direct manner when the boss is in the room can be difficult, particularly if the content of the conversation is controversial or risky. If the manager has a strong point of view about a subject, subordinates take refuge in agreement. If subordinates want to disagree, they are careful to tread lightly. Best to ease into it, rather than put oneself out there on an island. "Easing into it," as it turns out, is difficult to execute with direct language. Usually, extra words are inserted in the hope to find the right ones. We tiptoe around the message. In the worst case we babble. Nobody likes a "yes man," yet that is exactly the behavior rewarded and reinforced. In this context, it is easy to see how a staff that is eager to please does nothing but reinforce the prevailing points of view held by those in power. The managers had better be right, because subordinates find it too difficult to challenge them. It's just not worth the risk.

People in the workplace converse in ways that generally avoid traps. It's a natural reflex to protect oneself from prematurely owning a problem that may or may not occur. To outright own an issue, inclusive of all the ambiguity and uncertainty that comes with it, is very difficult for people, particularly when the culture is on a hunt for blame when problems emerge. Sometimes, people asking the questions are equally shy in anticipation of an answer they don't want. "How is the quarter going, Adele?" is a classic way for a CFO to ask a sales manager for an interpretation of performance to revenue goals. Adele has way too many ways to answer the question without really offering anything tangible. "It's looking great" might sound pleasant to the ear, but the content is vague and elusive. We simply have two happy people talking nonsense to each other. Is it a social opportunity to talk this way? Sure. But it is not communication of the sort we desire.

Delegation of Authority

Let's go back to my second observation I made earlier in this chapter about the other classic company behavior found so commonly. That is, the way employees act, interpreting corporate policy and processes with their rules of engagement.

There are two issues at play. The first, and perhaps intended factor, is one of compliance. It is a case of, "This is your role, and these are the rules." If people perceive their roles with a sense of strictness, expected to "stay within the guard rails," they will, in kind, stifle their appetite for daring actions to ensure compliance.

But unintended consequences follow in short order. If teamwork suffers, or the goals of the company are compromised by their actions in some way, so be it. Compliance to process, and rigid interpretation of delegation of authority, perceived or real, compromise the company's ability to respond quickly to circumstances organically. In essence, people are discouraged from problem-solving outside boundaries. Outliers, exceptions, and requests for outcomes outside the prescribed norm are ignored, dismissed, or passed on to another with minimum care.

The second factor is accountability. Here, in ways not dissimilar to those derived from Maslow's hierarchy affecting people's ability to communicate plainly, a strict delegation of authority dampens initiative. It can even breed complacency. It's a case of "be careful what you ask for, you might get it." Acting from fear for security and personal safety, people make damn sure they are not to be called out for misdeeds or errors that are "their fault." You want it done the blue way? Then, the blue way is what you are going to get, even if the customer asks for pink, or a colleague for yellow. Employers in this model motivate passive employee responses. Staff learn to be content to do their jobs, while generally decelerating organizational performance.

We Can Do Better

Peer-to-peer culture, with the underlying objective of underpinning a successful journey from small company to mid-size, must take these notions into account. Trust, team orientation, empathy, and honesty are necessary, as we have discussed. But there's something else we need to ensure if we expect crisp communication and initiative to work off-script in the best interests of the firm.

Let's call it: Dynamic action. Dynamic in communication and dynamic in decision-making. It is to be passionate in tone, urgent in approach, and efficient in delivery.

Merriam-Webster says to be dynamic is to be *"energetic and forceful."*[23] Frankly, I can't think of a better word than dynamic to describe the behavior we desire, though "straightforward," "authentic," "direct," "empowered," and "expeditious" all come to mind as welcome alternative descriptors. If I hold an aversion to BS, then our peer-to-peer culture had better call out BS as anathema.

Communication in peer-to-peer culture is dynamic. It is energetic in spirit and forceful in its clarity. We don't posture and we are not vague. Listeners must reject unsatisfying messages and ask the speaker to try again. It takes practice, but people do indeed get the hang of it. And what a difference it makes. Clarity of communication expedites understanding. Lack of posturing helps keep the team orientation intact. It is a constant reminder of how connected and codependent everyone is in the organization as true teammates in pursuit of group goals.

Decision-making in peer-to-peer culture is also dynamic. We hold people to account to behave in the best interests of the company, as they see fit, in the moment when an exceptional issue unfolds. We separate the fiscally responsible concept of delegation of authority (meaning certain people can spend $1,000 without approval, while others can spend $10,000) from the concept of doing the right things regardless of rank or role. In other words, we expect junior staff, though constrained within limits for spending on their credit card and purchase-order requirements, to make decisions in the moment as they relate to keeping schedules on track,

---

[23] https://www.merriam-webster.com/dictionary/dynamic

responding to customer problems, organizing teams, cutting deals, confronting conflicts, and a host of other issues as circumstances demand.

Are you a salesperson challenged to write a customer proposal and close an order? Collaborate and figure it out. Are you a project manager, just alerted to a key employee on sick leave and late shipment of a critical incoming widget? Collaborate and figure it out. Are you a marketing manager unsure how to introduce a new product concept to prospects? Collaborate and figure it out. In all these cases, we expect the peer-to-peer organization to behave with passion, urgency, and efficiency.

I know peer-to-peer culture is different from the typical firm in this way, as I have watched new hires join our company and find it difficult to subscribe to the behavior at the outset. "You mean you trust me to make these decisions?" Yes, we do. They simply need the opportunity and the support along the way. And over time, like dynamic communication, employees get better and better at dynamic decision-making. Yes, they make mistakes. But their will to succeed becomes so strong, it morphs into a sense of responsibility for participants. They own the process and the outcome, in a way they could not if the boss simply gave them the answer.

Dynamic Communication In Practice

To put it all into practice though, requires recognition of a few subtle points. First, direct, energetic, and forceful communication should not be confused with raising one's voice. Speaking in direct language has nothing to do with decibels. Nor does dynamic communication require someone to take a disproportionate slice of the airwaves in a conversation. We're not talking about folks who like to hear their own voices, lecture others, or get up on soap boxes. In fact, these are undesirable traits for a person exhibiting good communication skills. Verbal bullies need not apply.

Second, dynamic communication should not be dependent on the *way* people like to communicate. Folks tend to be wired as tell-assertive or as ask-assertive in their natural style of communication, as documented in a very useful model by TRACOM® Group.[24]

TRACOM® Group's SOCIAL STYLE Model™

	Analytic	Driving
	Amiable	Expressive

Controls
Responsiveness
Emotes

Asks — Tells
Assertiveness

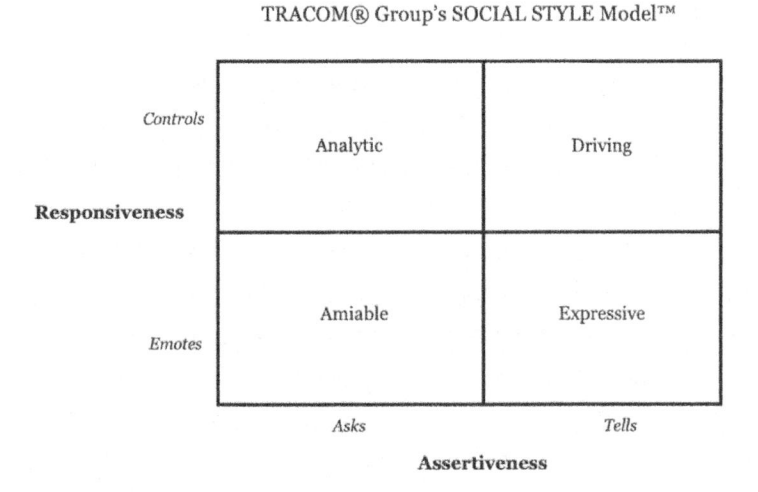

Figure 26: TRACOM® SOCIAL STYLE Model™

---

[24] https://tracom.com/social-style-training/model. SOCIAL STYLE is a TRACOM® trademark.

Whether at home or in the workplace, people more often than not communicate in one of these two patterns, consistently.

A tell-assertive person is comfortable directing others to think and do in a way they desire. Phrases such as "you should" are popular with this group. Depending on their relative style of responsiveness, tell-assertive people can have a driving style demonstrating a strong control instinct, or an expressive style exhibiting more emotional behavior.

Ask-assertive people are comfortable making requests and suggestions in order to direct others to think and do in a way they desire. Phrases such as "could you" are more often used. Those prone to control are labeled "analytic style," while the more outwardly emotional are "amiable style."

It turns out that both styles of ask/tell assertiveness can be equally accomplished by people striving for dynamic communications, independent of where they reside on the curve of relative responsiveness. Style, in and of itself, has absolutely nothing to do with effective communication. But we must be careful that the tell-assertive people in a peer-to-peer culture don't inadvertently gain unwarranted advantage in debates simply because they appear to be more confident in their delivery.

Labels and buzzwords, when used in moderation, are useful to help communicate complex concepts. The peril lies in this question: Do people understand the complex concepts, or do they just recognize the buzzword? It becomes disastrous when different people who *think* they know their way around a buzzword entertain different understanding from their peers about what exactly the buzzword means.

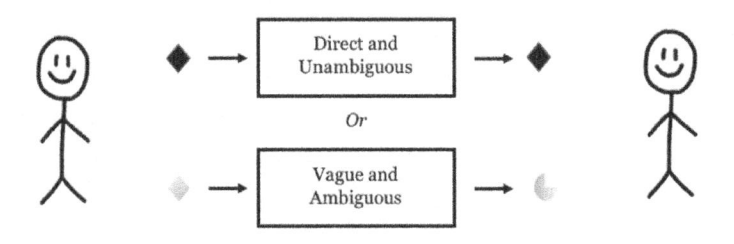

Figure 27: Direct Communication

In the worst case, nobody has defined the word, perpetuating an ongoing awkward game wherein no one wants to admit they don't know the meaning. So, we carry on with the discussion, in the absence of any real understanding. The best people can do is look for clues in what others say and put the pieces together the best they can. Or they find buddies in the hallway after the meeting and ask for mutual clarification and understanding.

Dynamic communication in a peer-to-peer culture avoids labels and buzzwords, as well as ambiguous language, high-order concepts, and passive sentence constructions.

That is not to say that certain words and phrases that are germane to the industry or specific technology are banned. A company-wide vocabulary shared by the staff is important and can be very helpful in grounding the protocol for plain speaking.

But complex concepts should never be dismissed with a word or phrase. Instead, staff are well served to dissect complexity into smaller, less complex subsets. If we are talking about "leads," for example, let's be clear whether we mean names of unqualified prospects from a Google search, qualified sales opportunities from conversations, respondents from surveys, or something else. And for certain, these "leads" cannot be conflated as one, cohesive entity. They are different and should be counted as different.

Posturing Must Be Corrected

Leaders of peer-to-peer culture must proactively correct anyone who engages in excessive self-promotion and posturing. On more than one occasion I have (again) used the sports team metaphor with employees who have strayed. I tell the tale of the soccer team, playing a very competitive game, that is losing at the halftime break by a score of 2-1. In the locker room, a passionate debate breaks out between coaches and players. Are the defensive formations the ones we should sustain forward, or perhaps do we change it up in the second half? Are we playing too conservatively in the midfield? Communication is direct and clear throughout the conversation when suddenly, a player interrupts and says, "Yeah, and did you see the shots I got off on goal? I am really beating my man today." In this context, it is an inconceivable scenario. In hearing the story, the employee recognizes quickly how selfish and unhelpful the ego-happy player is and sees himself in the tale. Posturing by an employee in a corporate setting is no more ridiculous than posturing by a player. Yet, we have all seen it. It is debilitating and a direct threat to teamwork. It has no place in a peer-to-peer culture.

Dynamic Decision-Making In Practice

The peer-to-peer organization yields tremendous advantages when behaving with a dynamic sense of urgency. Perhaps foremost, we want to render decisions expeditiously. Sure, the "best decisions" are only truly judged in hindsight. But by nurturing a culture whereby the best available information is considered, as expressed by the best available opinions both consenting and dissenting, without regard to personal penalty, the best decisions do indeed come forth. Employees are invariably smart. They know what to do. They just need the opportunity.

The management level of the organization can, obviously, have a great impact on employee behavior. It is a matter of encouragement and empowerment. But management in peer-to-peer organizations is always there to teach, assist, and respond to pleas for help. Sometimes, employees feels apprehensive, for whatever reason, and need reassurance. Perhaps the stakes are high, or the employee doesn't feel like they have the best information to make the decision. No problem. Management can help. But in these scenarios, there should always be a teaching moment for the person in the line of fire, so that next time they are confident and free to make the right decision, as they define right. Our goal is for everyone to feel comfortable making decisions in the moment. It is how we scale to mid-level success.

In Sum

- People don't speak plainly and clearly in the workplace. They fill the air with repetitive phrases, code words and acronyms.

- Posturing, when done to excess, is the work of the narcissist. In peer-to-peer culture, this behavior presents a real problem and must be corrected through rehabilitation or removal.

- If people perceive their roles with a sense of strictness, expected to "stay within the guard rails," they will stifle their appetite for daring actions to ensure compliance.

- Acting from fear for security and personal safety, people make damn sure they are not to be called out for misdeeds or errors that are "their fault."

- Peer-to-peer culture requires dynamic communication and dynamic decision-making. It is to be passionate in tone, urgent in approach, and efficient in delivery.

- Dynamic communication in a peer-to-peer culture avoids labels and buzzwords, high-order concepts, and passive sentence constructions.

- Employees are invariably smart. They know what to do. They just need the opportunity to exhibit dynamic decision-making.

Structuring the Peer-to-Peer Organization

Ask anyone currently employed about their reporting structure. Without hesitation, they will cite chapter and verse about their management chain, peer structure, and tree of subordinates and near subordinates. Org charts are littered with titles such as "senior market research analyst" and "vice president, retail banking" to offer people not just a role but also recognition.

And it matters to people. Just attend a holiday party among friends or a family reunion to hear the declarations of ego in the form of title. "Yes, Aunt Louise, I am doing very well in my career. I am now a senior support specialist at Acme." Aunt Louise is impressed and offers praise and approval, leaving no doubt. "Tommy is doing so well," she relays to her sister at the punch bowl. "He has been promoted to senior something or other at Acme. It is exciting. I always knew he would be a winner at the office."

Although occasionally undocumented, a company's org chart is a central element of the firm. In fact, bigger firms devote substantial portions of their org chart to, well, managing their org charts.

Those with management experience would argue there is little choice but to assume a benign structure composed of generic roles when building an architecture for operational execution. Managers define these roles, professed to fulfill duties critical to the firm's well-being. On paper, the roles look like chess pieces. The problem, of course, is it is real flesh-and-blood people who are called on to fulfill these roles, acting out the parts as best they can. Thus, there is usually a gap between espoused theory, as represented by published org charts, and actual behavior in day-to-day operations. In other words, the roles as drawn up don't necessary equate to behavior in the wild.

In books about sales methodologies, sales personnel sometimes are explicitly advised to find the "power base" in order to gain real understanding of how a potential customer operates, independent of what the org chart says. Jim Holden's popular book *Power Base Selling*[25] offers a good example. The premise is simple: Organizations don't work the way they are drawn up on paper. The map, in other words, does not correlate to the territory. If a salesperson with a little encouragement from a self-help book can figure it out, why do management teams put up with the dissonance between organizational behavior as intended and behavior in action?

Structure With a Purpose

Organizational charts are not, in and of themselves, the culprit. In peer-to-peer culture, we still need structure. Teams reporting to bosses who in turn are reporting to bigger bosses is a perfectly acceptable organizational paradigm, even desirable. People generally find it satisfying to have a place on the org chart to call home. The matter in question, of course, is how we get all the people to work together, to do the things required to achieve corporate goals with the highest

---

[25] Jim Holden, *Power Base Selling: Secrets of an Ivy League Street Fighter* (John Wiley & Sons, Inc., 1990)

efficiency, reliability, and intrinsic satisfaction for the participants.

In structuring a team in peer-to-peer culture, then, we must achieve two distinct outcomes.

One, we need a structure whereby our employees' personal sense of belonging can be fulfilled. Some want to puff out their chest and speak to their Aunt Louise of their place in the organization with confidence at the holiday party. Most simply need to continue to build out their personal résumés with the right titles and roles such that, down the road, they are well placed to step into their next career opportunity. Regardless, the titles must scratch the itches of individual needs.

Two, the structure must help resolve the dissonance, as described above, between espoused theory and behavior. Roles can be defined, along with the lines and boxes, on the org chart. But we need real behavior to unfold from these roles that is consistent with our desire for trust, teamwork, empathy, honesty, and dynamic communication and decision-making.

The secret to structuring a peer-to-peer organization is found in the fundamental understanding that functional groups rarely maintain the depth or breadth to achieve a corporate objective outright. It's just plain lazy to presume that the sales organization is responsible for generating revenue, the marketing department is responsible for branding and demand creation, the support desk is responsible for answering customer queries, and so on. Corporate objectives are not easily chopped and diced into neat little functional piles. By definition, corporate objectives are contemplated in the whole and achieved only by cross-functional execution.

So, in a peer-to-peer organization, we install a structure reflecting the aspirations of the firm in the aggregate. It starts by precisely defining the corporate objectives. For example, we may have total revenue, revenue by product type, and contributed margin by territory as the key parameters we are chasing this year, as directed by the board on behalf of shareholders. Undoubtedly, each of you reading can reflect on your own, unique goals. Whatever they are, define them with clarity.

Subsequently, we define roles that are indeed functional in nature. In the case of a company selling products, for example, the product development department is home to people who have particular skills in development. They spend most of their day, in fact, developing products. But that's not why they come to work. They exist, as names tied to roles in boxes on the org chart, because they are assisting the company to achieve top-level goals of revenue, revenue by product, and contributed margin by territory.

"This is mad," you may be thinking. "Why would we ask our product developers to consider their identity as citizens connected to goals such as revenue and contributed margin in the territories? Isn't that the job of the sales department?"

Herein lies the secret for success as a peer-to-peer organization. Everyone in the company identifies as corporate citizens first. The roles themselves are subordinate, as employees identify as functional citizens second.

Don't Confuse Roles With Behavior

Curiously, the roles, as we define them in peer-to-peer, look a lot like those defined in other firms. We indeed *do* employ salespeople, marketers, product developers, financial analysts, service managers, warehouse managers, and a host of other familiar functions. But unlike other firms, we maintain two important distinctions. One, we recognize that virtually all work worth doing requires cross-functional collaboration and cooperation. Two, though we hire people with specific skills to offer specific functional contributions, we ask them to assume both leading and supporting roles in the greater collaborative scheme of corporate cooperative work.

Let's look first at cross-functional cooperation. In peer-to-peer organizations, everything starts with, and flows from, the corporate objectives. Then, we identify the most important workstreams required to achieve a successful corporate outcome and install them as cross-functional initiatives. Cross-functional initiatives should be debated and established each year as deemed necessary to achieve corporate goals.

Sometimes an initiative is very specific, with a scope in time, such as a new product introduction (NPI). The corporate objectives measured by revenue by product line may hold the NPI as extraordinarily important and strategic to the future success of the company. It takes all departments, from product development to marketing to sales, to pull it off.

But there are other initiatives, not necessarily tied to a specific time frame, that are also important to achieving corporate goals. Take, for example, an initiative focused on customer service and satisfaction. Companies need to take care of their customers with maximum satisfaction at the lowest cost. To do it successfully requires an initiative coordinated between sales, marketing, service, and probably other departments as appropriate.

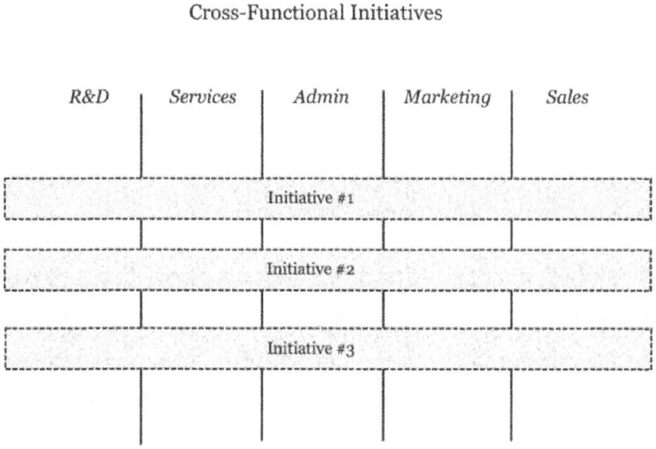

Cross-Functional Initiatives

| R&D | Services | Admin | Marketing | Sales |

Initiative #1

Initiative #2

Initiative #3

Figure 28: Cross-Functional Initiatives

In peer-to-peer companies, we install a system of leading and supporting roles to carry out these initiatives. Consider an initiative of improving the efficiency of acquiring new customers. The marketing department, in this example, may take the lead role for generating leads, to some standard of quality, at some volume, within some cost constraint. The sales department, then, plays a very important supporting role to define what, exactly, constitutes a quality lead. They help define the volume necessary to satisfactorily feed their sales funnels. And they provide a feedback loop so that quality and volume can continue to be optimized within the cost constraint.

The sales department then takes the lead on advancing prospective customers to closed customers, in some volume, at a minimum standard of quality, within time and cost constraints. Marketing plays a supporting role to provide air cover, website content, and PR to enable a swift and expeditious sales cycle.

Neither sales nor marketing, in this example, have the right to dig in and cite functional metrics to avoid accountability to the team and the initiative. Finger-pointing is taboo in peer-to-peer culture. If the initiative of acquiring customers goes unfulfilled, it really doesn't matter if marketing singularly or sales singularly did its part. The team failed.

In a working peer-to-peer culture, there is no way for marketing to succeed in this cross-functional initiative while sales fails. The initiative trumps the function: either it succeeds, or it fails. And if it fails, the entire team responsible for the program is implicated in its failure, and its rehabilitation.

It is likely that the same resource assigned to a specific job classification, such as "senior warehouse manager," will play multiple supporting roles along with one or two primary roles in the overall set of corporate initiatives. This is by design, and forces employees to consider their day-to-day contribution in a bigger context. They don't just practice their craft and "do their job." They go to work to support the initiatives and, ultimately, the goals of the company.

One of the appealing benefits stemming from the installation of initiatives, fulfilled by staff assigned to both leading and supporting roles, is how teamwork ripples through to the customer. The customer enjoys a relationship with their peer-to-peer vendor, perceiving them as one whole cohesive organization. For example, consider how many companies implement pre-sales and post-sales processes. Usually, the resources assigned to each are different. It makes sense. Call it a simple division of labor. The org chart lays it out: This group of folks need to tend to the efforts of a sale. And upon completion, they need to move on to the next set of opportunities and pass it over to the post-sales team.

The problem, of course, is the integrity of the handover. Too often, customers are left holding the bag as the sales team moves on a bit too abruptly. The post-sales team, new to the customer encounter, pushes the reset button on the relationship. "What did they sell you, again?" mutters the service consultant. In the worst of cases, the post-sale team initiates an apology session containing such catch phrases as, "I'm not sure the product was designed to do that." Many firms attempt to abate the issues inherent in handovers by installing information systems and other technology. Sometimes it works. Sometimes it doesn't. Customers are keen to share their stories on both sides of the debate.

Peer-to-peer organizations make a different statement about customer care. Yes, we still have division of labor. But the pre-sales team and the post-sales team are in fact, on the same team. The attitude is different, as is the behavior. It is in everyone's interest to ensure a smooth hand-off, following the guidance set forth in, for example, the customer satisfaction initiative. Inviting post-sales personnel to the table in advance of the sale is encouraged, every bit as much as permitting pre-sales staff to remain engaged with the customer after the purchase. It is all in the name of doing the right thing.

Compensation Is the Key

Managers, investors, analysts, and consultants have long argued that one's salary, in and of itself, is not a strong indicator of performance. In other words, what is a big deal during the hiring phase of employment is not such a big deal once the employee accepts the job and remains with the firm for a while. Everyone likes a raise, and lots of attention is paid during the annual review process. But in the other 11 months of the year, staff tend to pursue their jobs without a lot of thought about pay.

The manner in which most people are compensated is fixed, characterized by a salary paid by the month or a wage paid by the hour. Sometimes there is a bonus as part of the comp plan, paying out based on personal or departmental contributions. And of course, the company bonus is popular in cases where management strives to connect corporate performance to personal payout, usually reconciled annually. All these schemes are familiar to us and accepted as conventional.

The way we pay salespeople, though, is typically different. In many firms, a sales team is paid based on a total compensation, or T-comp, composed of a fixed and a variable portion. In fact, it is not uncommon for pay schemes to base a large part of the package on the variable component, such as 50% or even higher.

Typical Corporate Pay Plan

Salespeople

Bonus
Individual Variable
Base Salary

Everyone Else

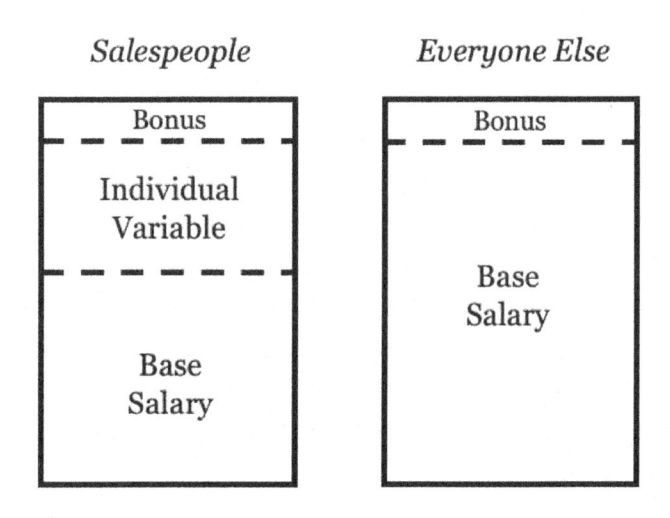

Bonus
Base Salary

Figure 29: Common Pay Plan

Why are salespeople often paid in this part salary, part commission style? Well, two reasons are generally accepted. One, to *motivate* behavior. The more one sells, the more one makes in commission, in most schemes. Salespeople love to make money. Two, to *focus* behavior, within a set of constraints, on the task at hand. A "territory" is assigned to the salesperson, creating the constraints. The pay plan, with its eye on the prize called "quota," then offers a direct connection to what precisely he or she is to do. Tie the pay plan to revenue, margin, or anything you like. Salespeople will respond like Pavlov's dog and do whatever it is you want them to do.

Now, go back and read these four paragraphs again. At one level, it all reads like something out of fifth-grade social studies class. You're thinking, "Duh, everybody knows this."

But consider the buried contradictions. First, for salespeople, we accept that specific, targeted behavior can be tied to, and even motivated by, substantial variable compensation in the form of commission ranging from 40% to 50%, or even up to 100% of the pay plan. For everyone else, we generally don't believe in that sort of scheme. If you do your job particularly well, you might get a reward as a sweetener, or perhaps a share in some company-wide payout as a bonus at the end of the year. But essentially, a job is a job. Just do it, please, for a fair salary or per-hour wage.

Furthermore, consider a contradiction, along the lines of, "Be careful what you ask for, you might get it." We tell salespeople to hit their quotas and pay them handsomely to do it. The corollary, though, is they are prone to take the direction literally. They focus on *their* sales campaigns with all their might, with much less attention to the tasks, deeds, and needs of others. "New-hire assimilation? That's somebody else's job. Sorry. Can't help you, even though I know a lot about sales around here. Other salespeople not doing as well? Sorry, can't help them either." In fact, if a competitively minded salesperson is honest, the sentiment will even stray to, "It's good they aren't doing as well, as it helps secure *my* trophy for top salesperson in the region."

It's not just salespeople. Other employees suffer the unintended effects from their own literal interpretation of their compensation packages. Fixed pay plans, or those with modest bonus components, can provoke lethargy and apathy among the staff. The bonus, if in play, can be perceived as too modest in amount, or more often, too intangible if payout is reserved for year end. The direct connection between bonus and behavior lacks the intensity of a commission scheme.

Of course, there are plenty of salespeople who behave unselfishly. But too many do not. And there are oodles of employees, paid a salary, who make outstanding contributions, working long hours, reaching beyond the strict parameters of their job description. But too many do not.

Getting It Right

In peer-to-peer companies, pay plans are constructed to maximize a causal connection between incentive, behavior, and reward for defined outcomes for all employees, while minimizing the contradictions held in compensation programs of the status quo. We do this in two ways.

The first borrows from the lessons learned in pay plans typically reserved for sales personnel. Everyone in the company is paid in a commission-like scheme. In other words, variable compensation is a substantive part of their individual plans.

It is paid monthly, based on parameters that are scored monthly. What constitutes "substantive" is judged manager by manager, role by role, but never less than 10% of the T-comp. First-line managers, for example, should be 25% variable, or higher. Executives should be at 40% at a minimum. But at the end of the day, *everyone* in the peer-to-peer company maintains an unambiguous and immediate link between outcomes and pay.

The second principle echoes our desire to install teamwork as a standard matter of course. So, we construct the variable portion of the pay plans such that the scored parameters are team-based. For the administrative staff, service personnel, marketing team, and others, this is a straightforward implementation. They are keen to behave to the call of team goals and be paid in kind.

Peer-to-Peer Pay Plan

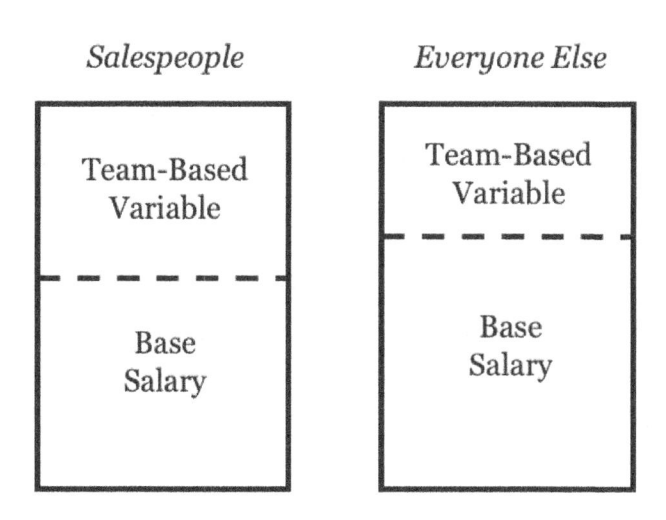

Salespeople   *Everyone Else*

Team-Based Variable	Team-Based Variable
Base Salary	Base Salary

Figure 30: Peer-to-Peer Pay Plan

Sales staff, though, based on experience at previous career stops, and more accustomed to individual plans emphasizing quotas, territories, and individual achievements, are asked to participate in the same team-based pay plans as the rest. In other words, in peer-to-peer companies, we treat sales staff the same way as others. We ask them to help achieve team goals, consistent with corporate objectives, and be paid based on achievement of these team goals. Again, the actual variable percentage is judged manager by manager, role by role. But 40% to 50% variable should be assigned to sales staff, as a general rule.

The team-based pay plan serves as the ultimate "put your money where your mouth is" representation of management's desire for the right behavior by all employees. Paying all staff on the same criteria, in the same way, ensures alignment, not just in the abstract but in pragmatic terms day-to-day. Administrative staff are more inclined to take notice of an email thread highlighting a customer concern when they know that revenue directly impacts their paycheck each month. It's not just "the sales department's job" to achieve results. It's everybody's job. Similarly, service managers encountering customer satisfaction challenges find more cooperative sales staff eager to attend an after-hours meeting to explore resolution.

The immediacy of the monthly scored parameters, tied to paychecks, make it work. And basing the scored parameters on team-based goals consistent with corporate objectives unleashes collaboration and cooperation across the peer-to-peer organization.

In Sum

- People generally find it satisfying to have a place on the org chart. The matter in question, of course, is how we get all the people to work together to achieve corporate goals with the highest efficiency, reliability, and intrinsic satisfaction for the participants.

- In the peer-to-peer organization, everyone in the company identifies as corporate citizens first. The roles themselves are subordinate, and employees identify as functional citizens second.

- In peer-to-peer companies, we install a system of leading and supporting roles to carry out cross-functional initiatives.

- In peer-to-peer companies, pay plans are constructed to maximize a causal connection between incentive, behavior, and reward for defined outcomes for all employees.

- The team-based pay plan serves as the ultimate "put your money where your mouth is" representation of management's desire for the right behavior by all employees.

Managing the Peer-to-Peer Organization

Corporate policy is widely considered a necessary component of any firm's existence. A peer-to-peer organization is no different.

A key component in good policy, of course, is to ensure the organization operates within the law. You would think that expecting people to behave within legal parameters should be taken for granted. But boards, and the investors they represent, can't be too careful. Many take an explicit approach, detailing specific behaviors that will not be tolerated. They delineate, among other things, hiring practices and policies covering discrimination, harassment, theft, and the treatment of intellectual property. Policy is clearly written such that anyone caught engaging in unlawful behavior has not, by definition, behaved consistent with the prescribed expectations and therefore is subject to disciplinary action up to and including termination. Thus, if people behave poorly, there is no misunderstanding about where the firm stands on the matter. It was the person, deemed an outlier, rather than the company, that should stand the burden of punishment directly. A peer-to-peer organization should publish policy to whatever level of detail it likes, relative to these legal issues.

But corporate policy usually goes beyond the strictly legal and enters into a collection of behavioral expectations for employees that are more about "corporate responsibility."

Here, the issue of litigation takes center stage, particularly in the United States, where civil tort law is an accepted element of business culture. Boards, and the investors they represent, don't want to be sued because of bad behavior by an employee. But as it turns out, boards don't want to be sued by investors either, for matters attributable to management malfeasance.

Publicly traded companies must be particularly cautious. One can imagine a naive employee tweeting to his heart's content about a product bug or a customer problem, triggering a stock sell-off, in turn leading to a shareholder suit alleging lack of due care in management discipline. No, best to have a policy for use of social media.

Indeed, the law and its companion, civil litigation, motivate clear, definitive corporate policy. So, declare intentions for how everyone is to behave and minimize the chances for misunderstanding about consequences. Keep the lawyers at bay. Simple enough.

But how far should one take this idea of policy as the ultimate protector? Should we legislate, with precision, how managers should buy stuff? How about dress code, using the business phone for personal calls, or "wasting time" with access to non-essential websites for news, sports, or entertainment on the company issued iPhone?

Some companies must be selectively rigorous. They are in a business, for example, in which dress code is important for its image to customers. Think uniforms.

But many organizations simply get carried away. And there are potentially dire, unintended consequences with all this prescribed documented policy. The field of psychology again provides a helpful lesson, this time from a practitioner by the name of Eric Berne. In his book *Games People Play,* Berne offers the theory of transactional analysis in which people take on parent and child personas as they engage in predictable patterns with each other.[26]

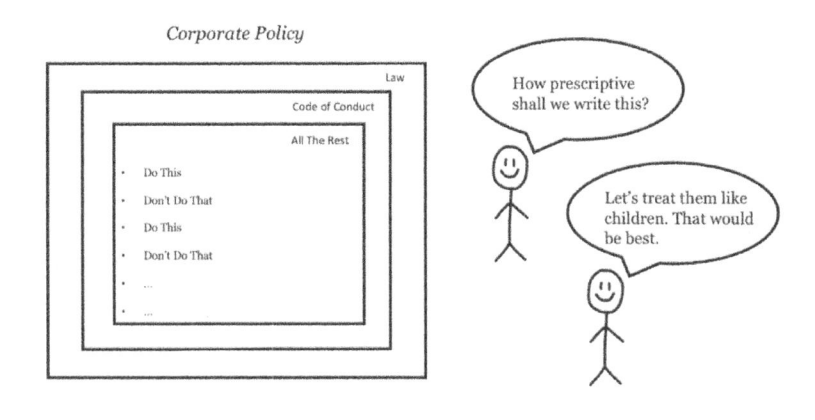

Figure 31: Common Corporate Policy

Human interactions ultimately progress to an outcome in which one party obtains a "payoff." In most cases, the participants are unaware they are engaging in this dynamic. But indeed, they are. Adults, as they morph into parents, gain

---

[26] Eric Berne, *Games People Play: The Psychology of Human Relationships* (Ballantine Books, 1964)

http://www.ericberne.com/games-people-play/

power over other adults, now playing the child. And as we know, children pout, sulk, and act out in all sorts of counterproductive ways.

Rigorous corporate policy puts the employer firmly in the role of parent. The employees, then, essentially engage in a parent-child relationship with their employer. And no adult covets this feeling, particularly at the office.

In practice in the workplace, people react in one of two ways. One, they game the system. Every rule is tested. Sick days are manufactured on sunny spring days. Creative writing projects ensue for expense reimbursement. Managers divide purchases into smaller pieces, so they can buy what they want while still remaining under their limits of signature authority. Like teenagers, employees will rebel. And these actions are routinely not aligned with the best interests of the organization.

Alternatively, employees accept the parent-child paradigm, and carry on with indifference. This is almost worse than rebellion. They do what they're told and stay out of trouble. And when an exceptional issue arises, ordinarily demanding swift organic thought, it is with little regret that they ignore their conscience and behave to the letter of the law. Again, the behavior routinely is not in the best interests of the organization.

In a peer-to-peer organization, wherein trust is such an integral component, we want to minimize the dangers that Berne warns us about. It is almost incomprehensible to, on one hand, declare a value of trust only to, on the other hand, prescribe a long list of do's and don'ts that go beyond reasonable protection from breaches of law and civil litigation.

Policy in peer-to-peer, then, should be written to protect but not to legislate day-to-day operating behavior. Treat employees as adults and expect adult behavior in return. Worrying about their propensity to misbehave is largely a waste of time.

Best Behavior, Not Best Practices

Those who have engaged in putting together toys for the kids in the holiday season know all too well that, if given a second chance, you would be able to assemble the plaything in a fraction of the time compared to the first attempt. We learn from blundering along, and the associated mistakes that come with it. There is no question about it. When it comes to assembling a new scooter, there are a bunch of bad ways to approach the endeavor, a series of better ways, and a best way.

Enthusiasts of industrial engineering practices in the 20th century will recognize the names of Frederick Winslow Taylor and Frank and Lillian Gilbreth, widely credited with the invention of the first time-and-motion studies used to break down human beings' approach to complex, manual tasks. [27] The quest is simple: Keep improving process for increased efficiency. Break up the bigger task into smaller pieces, then optimize the most efficient way of plowing through the

---

[27] https://www.encyclopedia.com/social-sciences-and-law/economics-business-and-labor/businesses-and-occupations/time-and-motion-study

smaller tasks, avoiding unnecessary physical movement and associated wasted time. In the end, a best practice is declared.

In business, of course, although tasks are indeed sometimes manual in nature, the predominant efforts are largely a mental exercise. And though we can't in most cases apply the literal standard of a time and motion study, we still crave the best practice. But how to choose one, as the dynamics of business are in constant flux? It's a difficult problem, as architects of a winning "best" practice want to assume a largely static set of conditions. As the complexion of the problem to be solved changes, the practice must be resilient, or it erodes in its effectiveness. How, then, does one optimize a process to navigate a fluid situation?

We tend to think about methodologies pertaining to marketing, sales, delivery of services, and product development disciplines as the formative components to create an illusion of reliability, and ultimately predictability. Sometimes, the process is simple enough, with sufficient repeatable parts, that a best practice can be deduced. Problems are often "modeled," so that we can treat the otherwise unstable situation more like assembling a scooter. Put the size 12 bolts in the holes in the frame first, then move on to the handlebars. Done and dusted. Many processes, such as in accounting, are of this sort. But many, many others are not.

Furthermore, the very nature of "best" suggests an end point or a destination. The danger is that, once decreed, best practices become entrenched. The risks inherent in declaring a singular best practice in a dynamic environment are clear.

Whoever came up with the practice had better be correct in their analysis.

In a peer-to-peer company, we accept the fluidity of the situations we encounter. Stuff happens. Stuff breaks. The unforeseen is perpetually visible only in hindsight. So, we don't attempt to engineer best practices, or worse, steal best practices as installed by larger firms.

We rely on our people. And we stay true to the five attributes of peer-to-peer culture. The emphasis, for the aspiring peer-to-peer CEO, is to focus on installing the five attributes of culture, rather than fixating on installation of best practices.

That is not to say that our staff, competent at their tasks, don't bring experience to the dynamic situation. They do. So, in that sense, what has worked well in the past is brought to the table. But the distinction is important. We don't attempt to manufacture *the* best practices in what we do, nor borrow them explicitly from others. We empower our people to behave organically, following the cultural expectations.

We demand the best behavior, rather than the best practice.

Managing Poor Performers

In a peer-to-peer organization, we always assume best intentions. We teach the principles of culture and demand that behavior, always, follow the principles. People, then, do whatever it is they need to in order to get their jobs done in the context of team goals. Peers, as much as managers, police the quality of individual contributions. It is a direct consequence of the team-based ideal that outlier behavior, when it occurs, is called out so efficiently. Nobody tolerates someone who is not making the appropriate contribution. It's easy to spot.

What does it mean to be a poor performer in a peer-to-peer organization? I have found that those having a difficult time, for whatever reason, are magnets for others eager to assist. It is in everyone's best interest for the individual to improve. So, let's help them. Peers almost always take the lead, offering counsel, training, or relief from a difficult task. When what's needed to fix the situation outstrips peer-level efforts, the issue is escalated to management. Perhaps roles can be reassigned, or tasks reorganized in some way to offer a solution. Maybe process must be re-evaluated to consider shortcomings and strengths of specific employees.

Managing Employee Performance

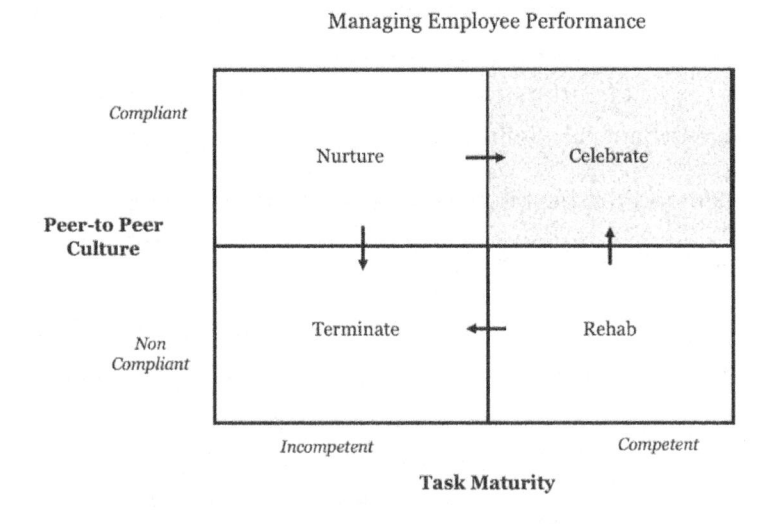

Peer-to Peer Culture	Incompetent	Competent
Compliant	Nurture	Celebrate
Non Compliant	Terminate	Rehab

Task Maturity

Figure 32: Managing Employee Performance

Whatever the solution, peer-level checks and balances, found naturally with abundance in peer-to-peer culture, usually save the day.

It is a rare case, but it does happen that an employee is a perfect exemplar of cultural expectations, but performance nonetheless suffers. Coaching, training, and other measures just don't help, and the employee is at a loss. It happened once to us during our three-year journey. Here, it is sad, but termination is the only option. It's just not fair to the rest of the team to carry a poor contributor, independent of cultural compliance.

But what if outlier performance is not just about task-level competency, but also a symptom of noncompliance with the culture?

In my experience, we've certainly had poor performers who, when confronted, resort to defensive routines and posturing. Sometimes people just can't get out of their own way.

Here, when performance suffers and compliance with culture is compromised, the decision is easy. We move aggressively to rehabilitate the outlier or exit them. There is no time to waste. And in this case, escalation to the highest levels of management can be very helpful. If someone on the team is misbehaving or ignoring any of the core principles, a senior manager or executive has the best chance to confront successfully. But if the effort to rehabilitate does not succeed, the employee must be terminated.

A more difficult situation arises when an employee is performing well at a task level but is noncompliant with cultural expectations. Do we put up with star performers, even

163

if they exhibit behavior that clearly breaks cultural norms? Managers in firms of all sizes face this problem. Often, star behavior prevails, and the employee carries on with impunity in these companies.

But in the case of a peer-to-peer organization, the answer is abundantly clear. We don't tolerate cultural noncompliance. Period. It is sacred ground. It is incumbent on everyone to maintain the cultural standard and escalate instances of improper conduct. Compliant employees must always enjoy a sense of trust for management to maintain the cultural standard. Management's job, then, is to act and act expeditiously. Fix it or exit the problem employee.

Career Paths and Voluntary Turnover

True commitment from employees is generally hard to attain for an employer that installs a culture anchored in personal goals, individual achievements, and singular accountability. Think about it. If you incentivize, reward, and punish people according to personal achievements, then what stops an employee from moving on to the next professional opportunity in which the perceived rewards are, perhaps, a wee bit larger? How do you manage the ongoing challenge to keep people satisfied if the criteria are personal in nature? Voluntary turnover inevitably follows.

The tragedy in this scenario is potential disenchantment felt by customers. All customers desire a relationship with a vendor that has a competent, stable workforce. When problems arise and misunderstandings surface, it is this competent workforce that works toward resolution. Startups thrive under this premise. When staff turnover increases, customers find incentive to shop elsewhere. Vendors must rely on the intrinsic strength of their products and services once customer relationships sour. I would go so far as to say that maintaining a committed staff that sticks around directly translates into a competitive advantage in the market.

A stable staff also offers continuity. Initiatives, workstreams, and campaigns that are started can be finished with the same staff. And as one initiative ends, the learning is retained as the next begins. Companies that maintain stable staff are at a competitive advantage over firms facing staff turnover. And when staff are satisfied, they tend to stay with an employer longer.

In the peer-to-peer company, the paradigm for managing employee satisfaction and involuntary turnover is materially different. Headhunters and competitors can try all they like but prying somebody out of a situation in which they experience the benefits of a peer-to-peer culture proves to be very difficult. It's not as simple as offering someone a $5,000 or $10,000 pay increase. Money, of course, is just one driver in a person's value system as they evaluate their employment. But once employees experience a peer-to-peer culture, they don't want to go back to the traditional ways of thinking or risk a change based on promises of loftier titles and responsibility unless they indeed are profound changes. Costly turnover is minimized.

But although we are in a team-based culture in a peer-to-peer company, we still must be attentive to the needs of each employee relative to their career. Transparency is the key. Employees must be encouraged to reveal their true aspirations, both near-term and far, such that we can provide the best level of support possible.

Through the process of managing a peer-to-peer company, I have found employees express all kinds of aspirations. When they trust you, they are free to tell you things about their desire to move to another state or another country. They might disclose a yearning to start their own business or change careers entirely. But most just want to progress in their learning, their contribution, and their compensation.

Peer-to-peer culture, founded in trust, promotes a cooperative engagement between employee and employer. We help them, the best we can, to achieve their goals personally. And wow, do they appreciate it. The whole affair grows on people, such that their commitment and loyalty accelerate.

Minimizing voluntary staff turnover is one of the hidden gems found in managing a peer-to-peer company. When staff are satisfied, they tend to stay longer. And when they stay longer, the firm enjoys tremendous benefits from the stability. Growing from a small company to one of mid-size is that much easier with a committed workforce in tow.

In Sum

- Corporate policy is widely considered a necessary component of any firm's existence. A peer-to-peer organization is no different.

- Policy in peer-to-peer should be written to protect, but not to legislate, day-to-day operating behavior.

- We tend to think about methodologies pertaining to marketing, sales, delivery of services, and product development disciplines as the formative components to create an illusion of reliability and, ultimately, predictability.

- The emphasis, for the aspiring peer-to-peer CEO, is to focus on installing the five attributes of culture, rather than fixating on installation of best practices.

- In a peer-to-peer organization, we don't tolerate cultural noncompliance. Fix it or exit the problem employee.

- In the peer-to-peer company, the paradigm for managing employee satisfaction and involuntary turnover is materially different. Headhunters and competitors can try all they like but prying somebody out of a peer-to-peer culture proves to be very difficult.

Hiring and Assimilation

One of the most vexing of all management challenges is to hire a staff. That is, to hire the *right* staff. We see some of the obvious ramifications as patrons in a retail economy. Coffee shops, restaurants, and the like live and die by their ability to place the right people on their teams. Customers vote with their feet, giving preference to the establishments that deliver a consistently good product and engaging service. Management ultimately relies on staff to perform their duties in the best possible way, consistent with the values and expectations of the business. Hiring the right people can make the difference between success and failure. It is costly, and potentially catastrophic, to make poor hiring decisions. Staff turnover is expensive and unproductive at a minimum. Consistent bad hiring practices can destroy a business.

So how do we find good people?

Consider again Andy Grove and his views about hiring in *High Output Management*[28]. Grove says it is important to assess candidates for two qualities, skill and will. Skill is about education and experience. Will frames one's desire to get things done, and a willingness to take on responsibility. The two together make up one's ability to do a job and successfully assume a role. It's not bad advice, coming from an industry icon.

---

[28] Grove, *High Output Management* (Vintage Books, 1983)

Others talk explicitly about "competency models," originally conceived in the context of testing in the 1970s by David McClelland at Harvard.[29] For example, the management consulting firm CQ Net describes the idea as that *"to be competitive, organizations should identify competencies necessary for successful job performance. A competency is an individual's demonstrated knowledge, skills and abilities, also called KSAs, that are demonstrated in a job context or particular organizational environment."*[30] Hiring for competency, then, requires qualifying candidates based on how they stack up against the model. The Society of Human Resource Management gives voice[31] to insights such as, *"Ask candidates to navigate hypothetical scenarios and explain or demonstrate what they would do in certain circumstances."* And, *"If we identify employees in advance for those competencies, we can reduce the chance of a bad hire and enhance the quality of hire."*

I have found, in practice, clinical approaches to hiring are deployed with varying degrees of intensity. In many cases, employers simply rationalize a hiring decision, based in large part on who they like, by raising the issue of "fit." Managers manufacture talk of soft skills such as "good communicator" or "hard worker" to define human capability beyond the task level. The debate at the conference table is resolved as the

---

[29] https://www.therapiebreve.be/documents/mcclelland-1973.pdf

[30] https://www.ckju.net/en/dossier/competencies-and-competency-models-what-is-it-how-professionals-benefit-competency-frameworks

[31] https://www.shrm.org/hr-today/news/hr-magazine/pages/0315-competencies-hiring.aspx

hiring manager concludes, "Colin and Tammy both look like they can do the job, but Tammy seems like a harder worker. And she has a great sense of humor. We can use some of that around here. So, all other things being equal, we should hire Tammy."

Maybe Tammy works out. Maybe she doesn't.

In peer-to-peer organizations, expectations for employee performance, of course, are different. We need task-level proficiency, but we demand cultural compliance. So, the hiring decision must fully contemplate these two critical dimensions. We must look beyond the attributes of skill and will, the theory of competency models, and the lazy loophole of subjective fit.

Peer-to-Peer Hiring Matrix

Task-Level Proficiency	Low Propensity for Cultural Compliance	High Propensity for Cultural Compliance
High	No Hire	Hire Unconditionally
Low	No Hire	Hire Under Condition of Growth

Figure 33: Peer-to-Peer Hiring Matrix

Cultural compliance, of course, is the most important dimension. If we can't predict compliance to a high level, the candidate cannot be hired, regardless of task-level proficiency.

If the candidate meets the standard for task-level performance, overlaid with cultural fit, the decision to hire is easy and without condition. But what happens if the candidate comes up short on task-level expectations, yet is a great cultural hire? It's a matter of risk, but one that should be assessed. Does the candidate show evidence that they, once hired, will grow to a minimum standard of performance in an acceptable time? If yes, hire. If no, don't hire.

Every firm will define a minimum standard and time frame in their own context but have likely hired plenty of people who were terrific cultural citizens, yet required training and nurturing to ascend to a desired level of performance. Because peer-to-peer culture is fundamentally crafted to motivate team performance, new hires short on proficiency but long on ambition and intelligence can grow quickly to meet the standard.

Task-Level Proficiency

Searching for task-level proficiency should be the easy part. But we have to be *very* careful that we qualify candidates based on their skills and aptitude, rather than relying on their expression of results, rewards, honors, trophies, and titles held in previous jobs at other organizations.

Candidates will, if given opportunity, trumpet themselves and their résumés. The tasks completed and the accomplishments achieved in the last set of job assignments provide the evidence, as they tell their tale, for future success. If they have done it before, they can do it again. Clearly, all these historical experiences have a context that are different from the set of conditions with the new employer. It is obvious. However, managers typically downplay the differences or ignore them outright in their quest to hire.

Sales managers provide a raging example, as they are notorious for hiring people based on labels such as "six-time quota club achiever," and "top salesperson in the region three quarters in a row." Did the candidate successfully sell widgets to information technology professionals in their last job? If yes, "They will perform well here at Acme, as we also sell widgets to IT customers." Never mind that in the last job, the "successful salesperson" maintained a star technical architect as a colleague, or represented a product caught up in a unique market trend, or possessed a particularly favorable territory and quota plan, or any number of other factors.

And the mindset is not limited to the search for sales personnel. Employers looking to fill roles for service, marketing, and administrative functions can all fall victim to this did-it-before, can-do-it-again prejudice. Candidates attempt to sway hiring managers with titles that start with "senior," statistics such as leads-per-dollar, and evidence of good fiscal judgment using phrases such as "always under budget."

The question for the candidate isn't, "What did you do?" It's, "How did you do it?" Task-level proficiency can only be assessed by an articulation of the steps one took, in the specific circumstances presented at the time. How did the candidate navigate market factors, colleague dependencies, management style, technology decisions, and the tools they had at hand?

On the heels of that is the question of why. Why did the candidate succeed or fail in a given situation? Why were they promoted to a title of senior? Why were they able to consistently meet schedules, exceed quota, or stay within budget constraints?

It is only through an understanding of how and why that a hiring manager in a peer-to-peer organization can hope to forecast with any reasonable probability that the skills and aptitude will translate to the new job. Interviews and reference checks should all be grounded in completing this understanding, as best as one can.

But task-level proficiency is just one dimension. The other, with elevated priority, is the propensity for cultural compliance.

Testing for Cultural Compliance

To test for propensity for cultural compliance, we must obviously first articulate to the candidate what peer-to-peer is all about. It should be effortless and routine for hiring managers to describe exactly what peer-to-peer culture is, and why it is crucial to the success of the organization. Just confess the truth: "We are not like the other companies you've worked for. We define ourselves by a peer-to-peer culture anchored in trust and teamwork."

The problem, sadly, is *everybody* says that. Managers in other firms, when talking to the same candidates, will describe cultural qualities using words such as trust, team, family, and customer-first. It is so easy to espouse. The candidate, then, is left to hear blah, blah, blah when *we* talk about many of the same qualities. The advantage for us in a peer-to-peer organization, though, is we don't simply espouse values, we install them.

So, when interviewing candidates, we must talk about the installment. Compensation plans are team-oriented, with a direct tie to company goals. Trust is given at the door when the candidate signs on, and we expect the candidate to trust others. Oh, and if there is a breach, you can be fired. I have found that graphic representation, using examples with the candidate, makes the point. We are, indeed, different from other companies. Each and every interview is going nowhere until the candidate grasps the magnitude of the matter. And as candidates go through their series of interviews with various company representatives, they get the message: "If you want to work here, you must possess a propensity for cultural alignment."

Once the candidate comprehends that peer-to-peer is, indeed, something different, the tables turn. We now have to assess their inclination, and their ability, to join the culture successfully.

Does the candidate value trust and teamwork? Ask them. Request examples in which they have been trusted and trusted others. Explore their point of view about team goals and team achievements in the context of their personal lives and career to date.

The problem we face is, again, one of game theory. Candidates want to impress. They position themselves in the best light, given the opportunity at stake. They embellish. They exaggerate. Some even lie. Somehow, we must break through.

I have found a strong correlation between the attributes we desire in a peer-to-peer organization and that of caring. By caring, I mean to be emotionally invested. Does the candidate care? About anything? It sounds like a stupid question. But for a candidate to successfully assimilate into peer-to-peer culture, they must care deeply about their craft, their contribution, and their place on the team. So, are they capable of caring at the level we will desire?

Intellectual Curiosity

If you ask a candidate, "Do you care about your job?" the answer will surely be affirmative. There's not much room for a more forthright response. But how do we really find out the true answer? By using a different phrase: intellectually curious. Tell the candidate that all the successful people we have in our company are intellectually curious. That is, they don't settle for surface-level understanding of things they care about. "What do you care about?" is an excellent question to pose. If blank stares come forth from the candidate, help them. "Do you like history? Do you like to ski? What, in real life, do you care about?"

The answer from the candidate might take shape as, "I love skiing. But I don't know much about the history of the sport or pay too much attention to the pro circuit. I just like to go up with my buddies and snowboard. It's a good time." He might even be thinking, "Why is she asking me about skiing?" This candidate is not your winner.

If a candidate is intellectually curious, that is, if they *care* about skiing, the response should be dominated by enthusiasm, while covering many of the aspects of the sport. If they care, it should be easy for them to talk in detail about the history of skiing, the evolution of equipment, the top locations around the world, the professional men's, and women's circuits, and how weather and snow conditions affect performance.

With this easygoing dialogue, the candidate has opened a window into the way they think, and their commitment to things in which they say they are interested. The precise topic the candidate chooses is largely irrelevant. Child rearing, interior design, cooking, fitness, travel, and gardening are all equally interesting topics to discuss with a candidate. Whatever spins their prop.

The right candidate will be not be vague. For those able to lock on to the spirit of the question, the ensuing answer becomes an unintentional disclosure about their level of intellectual curiosity and, ultimately, an indicator of their fit to peer-to-peer culture. The experiences that I and my colleagues personally enjoyed, in which we hired scores of people, substantiates the tactic as nearly flawless. It works.

You're Hired. Now What?

Once a hiring decision is completed, the next step is assimilation. We want the new hire to get off on the right foot, with enthusiasm. In theory, the new hire has the task proficiency to perform, and the propensity to comply with cultural expectations. But now, it's a matter of taking theory into action.

Here, the small firm, aspiring to get larger, is often hamstrung with a few "realities." Peer-to-peer organizations can find themselves underinvested when it comes to formal assimilation. Videos, manuals, and podcasts used by new hires to accelerate learning, so prevalent in large companies, are usually in short supply. You can't simply tell a new hire, "Read this and listen to that, and you'll be ready to go." And you certainly can't just throw them into the deep end and expect them to perform. To assimilate properly, a smaller firm must rely on human capital: its people.

As a starting point, let's recognize that the peer-to-peer organization maintains two advantages when it comes to bringing on staff. One, the installed culture can be espoused with clarity. Two, the specific cultural attribute of teamwork, supported by a team-based pay plan, motivates colleagues, bosses, and subordinates alike to take a stake in a successful outcome. It is in everyone's best interest to bring the new hire along quickly. The sooner the new hire makes meaningful contributions, the better for all.

Assimilation in peer-to-peer organizations is a five-step process.

1. CEO teaches culture.
2. Manager teaches role and sets expectations.
3. A sponsor/mentor is assigned.
4. New hire initiates their work.
5. New hire takes on the responsibility to ask for help.

To satisfy cultural compliance, the new hire must first be taught. Here, it is best for the CEO to take a personal role in the teaching. This is not something to delegate to a middle manager or a training department. It can be done in a one-on-one or a small group setting with multiple new hires sometime within the first few weeks of their employment with whatever props, slides, or Sharpie pens one cares to use. And as the CEO teaches the principles from the heart, with enthusiasm, the students experience their first emotional connection to the company. It's a form of organizational initiation. Nobody ever forgets it.

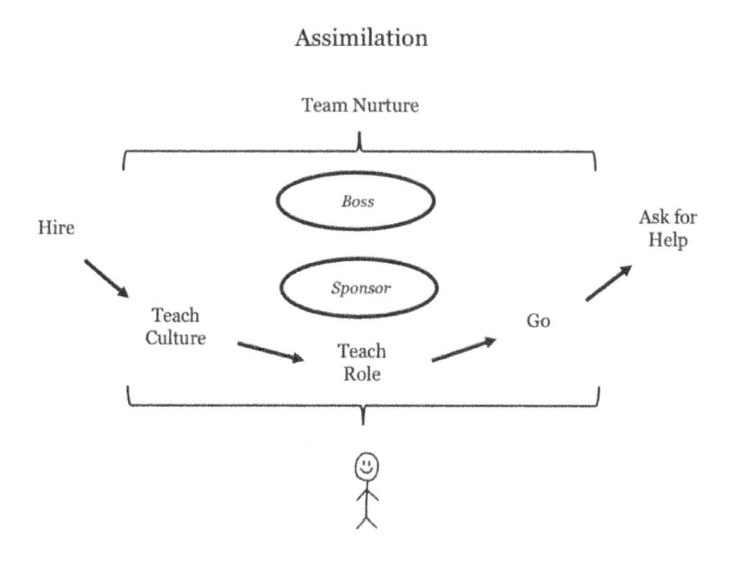

Figure 34: Assimilation

To achieve task-level competency, several people must come together. The manager, of course, is ideal to outline expectations for company goals, initiatives, and how exactly success as a company correlates to the pay plan. The boss is also in the best position to define the expectations for the role, and how the role leads, or is subordinate, in the context of key initiatives. With these two important pieces of information, then, the employee is free to explore their more specific to-do list.

A peer-level role model is also assigned. Think of this person as a mentor, certainly, but I prefer the word "sponsor." It is someone who knows how to do the job or has been, to whatever degree, doing it already. They will work side by side with the new hire. This peer-level role model is also an excellent source to advise the new hire on what to read, who to talk to, and what to study in their evening hours to accelerate their understanding.

The sponsor, by definition, is safe. The new hire leans on the sponsor for answers to any and all questions, without the perceived fear of retribution, or looking stupid. "Am I behaving correctly?" is a question all new hires have in the early days. Sponsors help new employees assimilate culturally, as well as settle into their role.

If you are lucky enough to maintain a staff of HR professionals, they can help immensely, offering counsel and training about what it means to be a citizen of the firm. And they can help formalize training as patterns develop and begin to produce the podcasts and videos I mentioned earlier. Their contributions are not to be understated.

But at the end of the day, the message to the new hire is, "Go. You have the skills to do the job. Ask anybody, anytime for help. But don't wait. Go. We need you to succeed."

I have found that a dive-in approach to assimilation is rewarding for all. Yes, the new employee makes mistakes. But there is little learning without doing. And with all of the helping hands, failure isn't an option. Do other employees, caught in the heat of the moment in doing their jobs, have difficulty finding time to help out new people? It's a logical question. But in truth, I have never seen it. No one in a peer-to-peer organization is incentivized or rewarded for personal contributions in and of themselves. All that matters are team results. Why *wouldn't* we help a new hire?

In Sum

- In hiring for a peer-to-peer organization, we must look beyond the attributes of skill and will, the theory of competency models, and the lazy loophole of subjective fit.

- It is only through an understanding of "how" and "why" a candidate performed in the past that a hiring manager in a peer-to-peer organization hope to forecast, with any reasonable probability, that their skills and aptitude will translate to the tasks at hand in the new job.

- Task-level proficiency is just one dimension. The other, with higher priority, is the propensity for cultural compliance.

- To assess someone's propensity for cultural compliance, test them for intellectual curiosity. What do they care about?

- Assimilation in peer-to-peer organizations is a five-step process.
    1. CEO teaches culture.
    2. Manager teaches role and sets expectations.
    3. A sponsor/mentor is assigned.
    4. New hires begins their work.
    5. The new hire takes on the responsibility to ask for help.

Extending Peer-to-Peer to Customers

Customers can behave badly. Really badly. Everything that goes wrong is the vendor's fault. Expectations for what the product or service is supposed to accomplish are boundless and perpetually unfulfilled. Statements made during the sales cycle, or perhaps written on the website, are taken out of context, months or even years later, as the basis for feeling wronged, ripped off, or victimized by broken promises. Threats of litigation can ensue. And with easy access to social media, trashing a vendor's reputation is easy enough to do.

But truth be told, I can only recall two customers who behaved from this frame of malice during our journey to mid-level success. We lost money in both cases. Were the customers conscious of their abuse, acting with purposeful intent? I'm not sure I ever figured that out, honestly. All I know is that we burned a lot of resources, acting in good faith, and attempted to resolve the issues as they kept coming up month after month. In the end, it was never enough. We looked to escape at the first available opportunity, contractually, while avoiding litigation and public trash talk on the internet. Eventually, we did.

The overwhelming majority of customers, thankfully, are not evil. But it is common practice for organizations to maneuver, connive, and manipulate others, all in the name of gaining advantage and, ultimately, winning.

What, then, explains the motivations behind their *mano a mano* approach to vendor relations that we observe with such pervasiveness?

Perhaps we can apply theories used by political scientists over the last century that help us comprehend relationships between nations. Do business entities, in the heat of the battle, resemble nations? If so, are policies and practices, deployed in business to gain competitive advantage, comparable to foreign policies practiced by diplomats?

Enter Hans Morgenthau, a 20th century "realist" political scientist of considerable fame at a time when World War II ended and the Cold War commenced. He observed that modern nations hold domestic traditions, beliefs, and experiences that bind them profoundly as a community. Their inhabitants, in essence, share, debate, agree and, when necessary, agree to disagree about matters that affect them.

Sounds like a business.

But nations throughout history, Morgenthau argued, have resisted collaborating openly with rivals to secure policies of trusted peace and shared interests. Think about the United States and the USSR during the Cold War, or the United States and North Korea in present day. Morgenthau raised a fundamental idea that international institutions, such as the League of Nations and later the United Nations were, in fact, *not* effective in matters of security and prosperity for participating states. *"To Morgenthau, the mistake [...] was to apply domestic experience to the international realm,"* writes author Barry Gewen.[32]

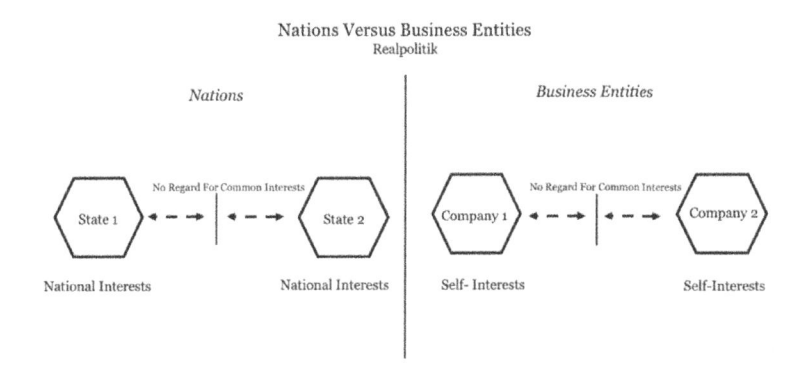

Figure 35: Realpolitik Comparison

An international community, he contended, simply does not exist in the same manner. In practice, nations look after their own interests for survival and power. Violence, or the threat of violence, is the backbone of effective foreign policy. It is the end that counts, and the end justifies the means. Simple as that.

Do businesses, then, maintain the same outlook (one of survival and power) within an "international community" of competing firms? Is the comparison accurate, or even fair?

I believe so.

---

[32] Barry Gewen, *The Inevitability of Tragedy* (W.W. Norton & Co., 2020)

One can certainly find military language as hyperbole in the workplace, such as "crush the competitor," as an expression of perfectly normal, acceptable sentiment. But would managers of a firm advocate, literally, an attempt of arson on the corporate headquarters of a rival firm or assassination of its leaders? Preposterous. Violence is out of the question. Would they attempt to collude with allies and fix prices in an attempt to run foes into submission? Tempting to some, but not possible in a lawful, regulated market.

Yet, to compete in business *is* commonly perceived as to survive and perpetuate power over others. Different song, same melody. So, firms must find other ways, free from criminality, to gain competitive advance at the neglect, or even expense, of other firms' interests. "Screwing others," in other words, becomes OK, as long as the end justifies the means, and nobody breaks any laws.

Too harsh? I think not.

The tactics are often opaque and not proclaimed publicly. CFOs, for example, find it perfectly acceptable to install clandestine payment policies with their suppliers that withhold distribution of funds beyond agreed terms to bolster the effects of cash management and quarterly results.

Companies also organize themselves to focus behavior on gaining competitive advantage. See "Exhibit A," the purchasing department. Here, staff is employed, at least on the surface, with good intentions. Maintaining a portfolio of vendors, each of whom must meet a minimum standard with respect to financial solvency, quality assurance, and security, is undeniably a worthy endeavor. Purchasing agents not only process the mechanics of buying decisions, they also assist with the goal to manage costs. So far, so good.

The problem unfolds when purchasing staff take unreasonable steps to extract the maximum in negotiations. Never mind that a deal was agreed to in good faith by line management. The vendor has to give more. The win-lose paradigm, all of a sudden, shows up. Sometimes, the line manager, director, or VP calls an end to the game and the agent relents. But often, not. It can become particularly problematic in situations where the customer is of larger size, exhibiting greater separation between the parties in purchasing and the line of business. Here, I have witnessed buying decisions drag out, under the guise of getting the best deal, in which deadlines and milestones critical to the business are dismissed and ultimately missed. Negotiation, when viewed as a contest, rarely offers a favorable outcome when all factors are considered. Yes, the customer might get a better price, but at what cost?

Overlay all this with history. Customers always have war stories to tell, describing how previous vendors have burned them, boxed them in, or otherwise compromised their ability to hit goals and manage their business. History leaves a scar. So, in the future, customers think and act so as to never be burned again.

But wait. There's more. Customers inevitably maintain purchasing processes with many steps. Often, multiple potential vendors are required to submit bids or engage in sales cycles to justify a fair and well-thought-out buying decision. Fair enough. But customers will often hijack a buying process to get what they want, while using other vendors to simply fill out the requirement for consideration. They seek free education about products, methodologies, and the competitive landscape of the market. For the superfluous vendors at the table, never to be really considered, it is an obvious waste of time and resources.

Customers, with all these factors, become conditioned to behave with their vendors, particularly the new ones, in a guarded manner. Best not to say too much. It is the "natural habitat" where customer-vendor relationships seemingly reside most comfortably. Guarded customer communication motivates vendors to also be on their guard in communication. Information is offered carefully or withheld, and posturing is accepted as the norm on both sides. Skepticism reigns like royalty.

Breaking the Spell

The obvious question, then, is can we work with customers to break the spell? Or posited more literally, can we mitigate the conditions that otherwise so strongly motivate guarded communication, the perception of a zero-sum game, and bad behavior generally?

I believe the answer lies in aborting the Morgenthau paradigm of survival and power, and in taking up a model of customer engagement supported by the assumption of widespread human morality and shared interests.

This idea, too, has a foundation in political science. Woodrow Wilson, the American president from 1913-1921, put forth an international policy at the end of World War I that essentially conflated human values with that of the state. Wilson argued that *"the state has no right to claim a separate morality from itself. Foreign policy should reflect the same moral standards as personal ethics.*[33] Wilson sought formal agreements with other nations, based on shared values and the pursuit of peace, enforceable by an international committee, the aforementioned League of Nations, despised by realpolitik thinkers such as Morgenthau.

If we perceive corporate entities as sterile institutions that seek advantage, however ruthless the acts, we are thinking like Morgenthau. To successfully extend the peer-to-peer organization to customers, we must think like Wilson.

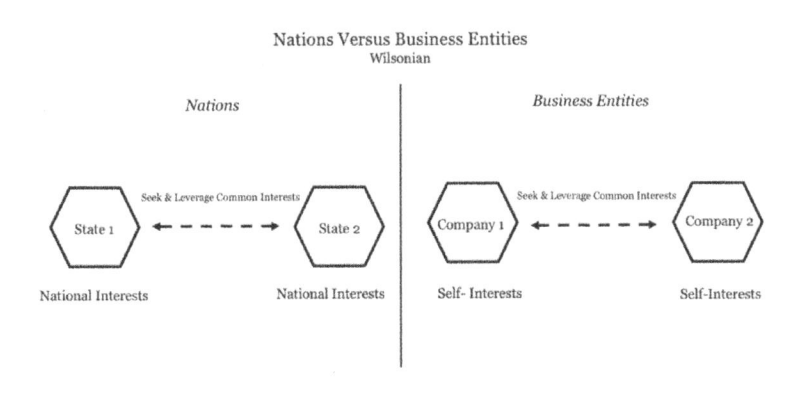

Figure 36: Wilsonian Comparison

Much of what defines the customer's behavior as experienced by employees is not necessarily rigorously legislated. The door is open, in many cases, for values such as empathy, honesty,

---

[33] Henry A Kissinger, *Diplomacy* (Simon & Schuster, 1994)

and trust to ascend, as long as the values themselves don't compromise a literal breach of expected corporate behavior. In other words, people carry with them a moral compass. It may just be hard to see when people assume roles in the corporate organization. The role says: Act in the Morgenthau model. The human underneath the role says: Act to a moral standard.

Take an example in which a middle manager, responsible for the successful implementation of a new project, is in the heat of contract negotiations with a supplier. The manager fears failure as much as covets success when contemplating the future of their project. Fear, then, motivates a plea for help. And such a plea is difficult to communicate successfully without some minimal level of expected trust.

The customer, if in the right frame of mind, can let their guard down, speak with more honesty, and behave with more openness to achieve results in cooperation with their vendor. They become free to say, "You'll have to finalize the details of the contract with the purchasing department. But I can tell you exactly what budget constraints we are under in formulating your proposal."

The peer-to-peer organization seeks to find and expose the moral compass of the human, living a layer beneath the assumed role, in customer interaction.

How?

We approach customers in a manner consistent with the same peer-to-peer attributes we hold in our internal culture. We take the lead, trusting that human morality will find its course in the way the customer responds and reacts. From the first encounter with a new prospect, we speak with direct and dynamic tone. We are honest and empathetic. We approach the relationship with a team orientation. And, last but not least, we trust them. Blindly.

Customers, as they interact with the peer-to-peer organization, are quick to see for themselves that this is *not* business as usual. What we espouse, as citizens of a peer-to-peer organization, is in fact the same as what we practice. We *say* that we trust them and then behave accordingly. We say we value a team orientation in our relationship, and then behave in a consistent manner.

Evolution of Customer Behavior

Consistent Peer-to-Peer Stimulus

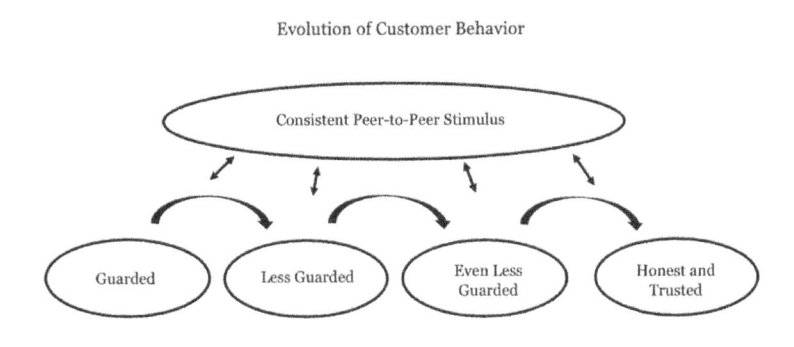

Guarded → Less Guarded → Even Less Guarded → Honest and Trusted

Figure 37: Evolution of Customer Behavior

When the peer-to-peer organization behaves consistently, customers have a way of letting their guard down. Trust doesn't happen in the first meeting. From the customer's point of view, it can be a risky proposition. People get fired all the time for making bad decisions.

But when we engage in trustworthy behavior at the outset, the customer grows in their trust, exhibiting higher levels of honesty in their engagement.

This can be particularly compelling in a mature relationship, for example, years after the initial decision to buy. When things are going well, managing a customer relationship is a piece of cake. But when exceptional issues arise, such as consultants not showing up to the job on time or a product that breaks, this is when the relationship must hang on its own merits.

Customers engage with their vendor through multiple points of contact, from accounting to marketing to the help desk. It is imperative that the staff of a peer-to-peer organization behave consistently across the entire spectrum. It's not good enough to trust blindly in the sales department. The accounting office must also trust, for example, when payments are late. The vendor rep must assume that no ill intent is in play and communicate with the customer empathetically. Same goes for the support hotline. Trust must be maintained throughout. One breach, and the customer relationship is damaged. More than one breach, and it all may bleed beyond repair.

Just Do It

A peer-to-peer organization externalizes all of its attributes.

We implement the give-get paradigm early in the relationship. Long before one could argue "we deserve it," we ask for things as we give things. We assume, if trust, empathy, and honesty are to form the foundation of the prospective engagement, that we can communicate with dynamic tone. We are straight shooters, right off the bat. We ask early in the relationship, "How do you guys buy stuff over there at Pesher Enterprises? Do you routinely spend out of hard budgets or do you have discretionary funds available?"

We exhibit dynamic decision-making. From the strength of peer-to-peer culture, we don't invent needless process and points of escalation for internal approvals to get something done. Let's do the right thing, no matter who is in the room, at every opportunity. It's not always a happy ending, but we can direct efficiency into the relationship and create safety for a customer. If the customer wants to buy from another vendor, for example, they simply say so.

Human morality may, in the end, not prevail. A customer is free to take advantage of the peer-to-peer organization. They can, and in fact do, sometimes engage in deceitful behavior.

But morality vacuums are rare. I have found that the overwhelming majority of the customers we have served appreciate a peer-to-peer approach and are eager to engage in the same manner. Good people with good character, who resonate with peer-to-peer values, are everywhere.

Partners: A Unique Challenge for Cultural Congruence

Most businesses rely on partners, in one form or another, for their livelihood. Sales channels provide access to customers. Of course, suppliers offer the key goods and services. And there are lots of influencers out there as well, potentially with the ability to refer, endorse, or substantiate the products and services that drive revenue.

And, oh what a joy it is to work with organizations who share even *some* of the values we practice in peer-to-peer. Much like with customer engagements, supplier relationships steeped in trust and honesty offer a tremendous advantage when things go awry. To approach a supplier with a problem within the backdrop of a team orientation is far better than to engage in an untrustworthy manner. Trusted sales channels offer the same benefits.

How, then, to extend the peer-to-peer organization to these partners?

It is not easy. And it may not always be possible.

We need a product from a supplier, for example, largely independent from the cultural attributes on display in the actions of people we come in contact within in the supply chain. We also need public relations, accounting, and other services in which vendors maintain competency. I think the best we can do is reward our suppliers who see the world the way we do, while remaining on the lookout for alternative vendors in the cases where cultural values are not shared.

Sales channels, on the other hand, tend to react to our peer-to-peer advances more like a customer. Channel partners, like all companies, behave within their own framework of culture, espoused or otherwise. But I have found reception to a peer-to-peer espoused culture, and an ability to mirror back many of the behaviors we practice.

Does that mean the channel partner practices peer-to-peer internally? Probably not, though in one case we were able to influence a channel partner to adopt many of the key elements of peer-to-peer within their own firm. Does the channel partner practice peer-to-peer with their customers? Again, probably not, with rare exception.

So, if the channel partner is not practicing peer-to-peer internally, nor with their customers, what's the point? Who are we, anyway, to push our value system on them?

Channel partners present a unique opportunity in that they represent a firm's products and services. A peer-to-peer organization, as perceived from the outside, maintains a particular brand simply because of the way they behave. Products and services aside, customers and partners alike desire to do business with a peer-to-peer organization precisely because of the attributes of trust, team orientation, empathy, honesty, and dynamic action. In the vernacular of the street, the channel partner "can sell that." It is an advantage, then, for a sales channel partner to use the brand of peer-to-peer when they represent their products and services.

It is satisfying to navigate the landscape of partners, knowing that, as a peer-to-peer organization, we maintain something unique. Differentiators can often be hard to come by in business, and even harder to sustain. To be reliably consistent in our behavior, we offer all who come in contact with us the chance to perceive us as different.

Indeed, we believe it is not just a matter of "different." We believe it is a matter of better.

In Sum

- Companies routinely organize themselves to focus behavior on gaining competitive advantage. See Exhibit A, the purchasing department.

- Customers become conditioned to behave with their vendors, particularly the new ones, in a guarded manner.

- Much of what defines a customer's behavior is not necessarily legislated. The door is open, in many cases, for values such as empathy, honesty, and care to ascend.

- Customers, as they interact with the peer-to-peer organization, are quick to see that this is *not* business as usual.

- Morality vacuums are rare. Customers appreciate a peer-to-peer approach and are eager to engage in the same manner.

- A peer-to-peer organization, as perceived from the outside, maintains a particular brand simply because of the way it behaves.

Epilogue

It continues to perplex me that the ideas that are fundamental to the peer-to-peer culture, borrowed from the school of common sense, are not seen more widely in practice. It is such an enigma. People, in their daily lives, generally subscribe to a system of morality defined by values. They certainly spend a lot of time ensuring their children learn the concepts. Right is right, and wrong is wrong.

Adults, though, are funny creatures. The laws of Maslow's Hierarchy seem to motivate behavior that, if their children only knew, would cause people embarrassment and even shame. The quest to gain an advantage, in the name of the best interests of the family, prompts all kinds of suspect behavior.

So, when the laws of human nature are applied to capitalism, I guess it should be no surprise that people behave with a variety of suspicious intentions. Customers try to get the better of their suppliers, while vendors manipulate prospective customers into buying things that they might not even need. Employees play games, incessantly, while managers ignore or participate themselves.

But I don't think people feel good about all this manipulation, if they are forced to think about it. They *want* to interact with others in a trusted manner. But greater societal forces generally warn us not to trust without a damn good reason, and certainly not blindly. Teamwork is a dandy concept, until employees realize that they are victim to political shenanigans and suffer real consequence. Honesty? Not at the office. It's all too risky.

Consider again the first few pages of Chapter One. Starting a small business is hard work. Growing is even harder. Yet more often than not, the best of human behavior shows its face along the way. There may be no better time, in fact, than when a business is in its first phases of growth to demonstrate some level of congruence between what people want and what people do. Trust, teamwork, empathy, honesty, and a dynamic approach to communication and decision-making are not crazy concepts in a young firm. And it all happens with a natural rhythm.

Entrepreneurs truly believe in what they are selling. Customers really gain material benefit from purchasing from small firms, else why bother? The big guys offer plenty without the risk. And when something breaks, leaders of small firms jump through all kinds of hoops to make sure the customer emerges satisfied. They have to. Their very business is at stake.

Just because a small business wants to grow and break into the $50 million club, why abandon the values that got you there? Peer-to-peer culture is about espousing, decisively, many of these same values. We declare them. We teach them. But espousing is not enough. We must put into practice a theory in action. So, we make a conscious effort to install these things and make them sacred. We say it, and we do it.

Prematurely rushing to look like, and behave like, larger firms is just a bad idea. This is an essential provocation I raise in this book.

Big companies, though well-grounded in policy and process, let linger the gap between culture as espoused and culture in practice. For a small company to grow up, there can be no gap. Say who you are and be what you say.

It is too seductive for a CEO, attempting to grow their firm to next-level status, to buy into all the hype about best practices, governance, prescriptive policy, systems, and spreadsheets. Don't do it. You will drown in detail while your staff struggles to understand the vague notions of the behavior you ask of them.

Inconsistency, misunderstanding, competition among peers, and office politics do not breed success. Nor do the implementations of stovepipe org charts, sterile processes fulfilled by roles, and a focus on individual incentive, reward, and punishment. CEOs know that businesses, particularly those aspiring to mid-level success, are only as good as their people.

We should require our people to perform at their best, in a reliable way, to sustain growth and meet the objectives as commanded by the owners. These objectives are, always without exception, held for the firm as a whole. So why not manage the people as one cohesive unit? Culture provides the means. Peer-to-peer culture provides the way.

Finding success does not come from the installment of best practices. It comes from the installment of best behavior. Behavior, as it turns out, is all that matters.

About The Author

Mark Budzinski is a management executive focused on the unique challenges facing leaders of small businesses. He has held an abundance of C-suite roles in the technology sector. He can be reached via email at markbudzinski@gmail.com.

Made in the USA
Monee, IL
21 July 2020